# As I Lay Dying
## stories out of stories

❡

Twayne's Masterwork Studies
Robert Lecker, General Editor

# As I Lay Dying
## stories out of stories

❡

*Warwick Wadlington*

Twayne Publishers • New York
Maxwell Macmillan Canada • Toronto
Maxwell Macmillan International • New York  Oxford  Singapore  Sydney

*Twayne's Masterwork Studies No. 102*

Copyright © 1992 by Twayne Publishers

Twayne Publishers
Macmillan Publishing Company
866 Third Avenue
New York, New York 10022

Maxwell Macmillan Canada, Inc.
1200 Eglinton Avenue East
Suite 200
Don Mills, Ontario M3C 3N1

Macmillan Publishing Company is a part of the Maxwell Communication Group of Companies.

**Library of Congress Cataloging-in-Publication Data**

Wadlington, Warwick, 1938–
As I lay dying : stories out of stories / Warwick Wadlington.
p. cm. — (Twayne's masterwork studies ; no. 102)
Includes bibliographical references and index.
ISBN 0-8057-8070-X (cloth). — ISBN 0-8057-8115-3 (paper).
1. Faulkner, William, 1897–1962. As I lay dying. I. Title. II. Series.
PS3511.A86A8658   1992

813'.52—dc20

92-18053
CIP

10 9 8 7 6 5 4 3 2 1 (alk. paper)

10 9 8 7 6 5 4 3 2 1 (pbk.: alk. paper)

Printed in the United States of America.

# contents

47145

# note on the references and acknowledgments

In *As I Lay Dying* Faulkner experiments with departures from convention at every level. His attention to detail results in unconventional punctuation (e.g., dropping the apostrophe in words like "ain't" and the period in words like "Mrs.," and using ellipses with 3 to 12 points), nontraditional typography (especially the use of spacing between words to suggest their resonance and rhythm, as in "Chuck. Chuck. Chuck."), unusual capitalization, and archaic but acceptable variants in spelling. As might be expected, this careful unconventionality has made it difficult to publish a reliable text, in the sense of one representing Faulkner's wishes at the time he revised proofs for the novel.

The edition used here is "The Corrected Text" of *As I Lay Dying* established by Noel Polk (Vintage Books, 1987). According to the "Editors' Note," the copy-text used is Faulkner's own ribbon typescript setting copy "emended to account for his revisions in proof, his indisputable typing errors, and certain other mistakes and inconsistencies that clearly demand correction" (243).

In accordance with the format of the Masterworks studies, the notes have been kept to a minimum. No one can write on this novel, however, without being aware of a debt to the existing body of commentary, which I gratefully acknowledge here. Among the items listed in the bibliography, I found James A. Snead's discussion of the novel particularly stimulating, and I drew several times on information provided by Dianne C. Luce's *"As I Lay Dying" Annotated* and André Bleikasten's *Faulkner's "As I Lay Dying."* Also informative and stimulating were conversations with Donald M. Kartiganer and John T. Matthews. Finally, I thank Elizabeth Harris, India Koopman, and Paul Wadlington for suggestions on my manuscript.

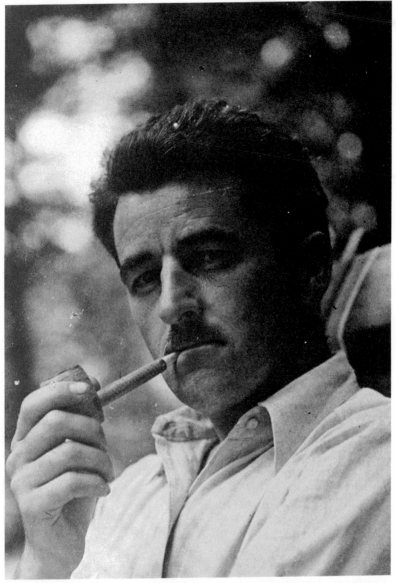

William Faulkner in 1931. Marshall J. Smith photograph courtesy William Boozer Collection.

# chronology:
# William Faulkner's
# life and works

c. 1841–1889 Faulkner's legendary great-grandfather, William Clark Falkner, arrives as a youth in Mississippi. He becomes a prosperous landowner, lawyer, and politician, serves as a colonel in the Civil War, builds a railroad, writes several books including a popular novel, and is killed by a former associate. As both positive and negative example, this ancestor plays an important role in Faulkner's imagination, representing one extreme of white social class as the Bundrens and their neighbors represent the other in *As I Lay Dying*. (In 1918, William Faulkner will restore the *u* that Col. W. C. Falkner dropped from the family name.)

1897–1903 William Cuthbert Falkner, the first of four sons of Murry C. Falkner and Maud Butler, is born in New Albany, Mississippi, 25 September 1897. Five years later, after the family railroad is sold, he moves to Oxford, Mississippi, his home for the rest of his life. His father, a rather ineffectual provider, for several years runs a livery stable, where William spends much time as a boy.

1904–1918 James K. Vardaman, the namesake of the youngest Bundren, after several terms in the state legislature leads the "revolt of the rednecks" as governor (1904–1908) then as U. S. senator (1912–1918). The

Falkner family supports Vardaman and like him cultivates a following among white small farmers such as the Bundrens. Although William's grandfather and later his uncle periodically hold state and local offices, the Falkners' real political power exists behind the scenes.

1914       Begins his friendship with Phil Stone, four years older, who plays mentor to Faulkner at the beginning of his career. Effectively drops out of high school but reads widely in classics and modern writing.

1916–1917  Works briefly as clerk in grandfather's bank, writes verse, and begins supplying drawings for the University of Mississippi yearbook though not yet enrolled.

1918       He and Estelle Oldham have planned to marry; instead, under family pressure, she marries Cornell Franklin. Faulkner enlists as a cadet in the Royal Air Force in Canada by passing himself off as British. The war ends before he completes preflight training, but for many years he misrepresents his war experiences. (Actually begins flying in 1933.)

1919–1925  For the first two years he is enrolled as a special student at the university, where he performs well in foreign languages but indifferently in English literature. Publishes poems, reviews, essays, and short stories in the student newspaper and in commercial periodicals, as well as a collection of poems, *The Marble Faun*. His poetry is derivative late-romantic verse, but his mature prose draws on its lyricism.

1920       Lee M. Russell, associated with "Vardamanism," is elected governor. Originally from the hill farming region where Faulkner will locate *As I Lay Dying*, Russell began his career in the law office of Faulkner's grandfather and is supported politically by the family. Two years before, Lt. Gov. Russell's influence helped get Murry Falkner a minor post at the university. A nouveau riche named Joe Parks, further evidence of somewhat greater white rural social mobility, forces Faulkner's grandfather to resign as president of his bank and takes his place.

1921    Works in a New York bookstore managed by Elizabeth Prall, who later marries Sherwood Anderson. Political connections win Faulkner his most notorious job, that of University of Mississippi postmaster, from which he will be fired after two years for grossly neglecting his duties in order to write and socialize with friends.

1922    Serves as chauffeur for his uncle John, who has been appointed district judge by Gov. Russell and now campaigns for election. In the rural areas witnesses the escape of half-wild "spotted" horses and collects other impressions to be developed in *As I Lay Dying* and elsewhere.

1924–1927    Henry L. Whitfield, whose last name foreshadows that of Addie Bundren's lover, serves as governor, having been elected with strong support from women.

1925    Faulkner lives in New Orleans January–June; associates with Sherwood Anderson and other writers and artists. Travels in Europe July–December, where he visits Italy, Switzerland, England, and France and lives in Paris.

1926    *Soldiers' Pay*, his first novel, prefigures *As I Lay Dying* by depicting a mortally wounded pilot and those affected by his slow dying. Hemingway's *The Sun Also Rises*, also focusing on postwar traumas, appears with its famous epigraph, credited to Gertrude Stein, that others applied to writers like Hemingway and Faulkner: "You are all a lost generation." After a long apprenticeship as a writer, Faulkner begins a remarkably prolific decade and a half: 16 books, numerous short stories, and work on a number of screenplays.

1927    Publishes *Mosquitoes* (novel), set in New Orleans.

| | |
|---|---|
| 1928 | Tries unsuccessfully to sell a "spotted horses" story entitled "As I Lay Dying." Again chauffeurs his uncle during his political campaign. |
| 1929 | Publication in January of *Sartoris,* later published in its original longer version as *Flags in the Dust* (1973); his first novel set in his home area. Like the previous two novels, it wins some respectful reviews but earns very little. In April Estelle Oldham Franklin is divorced. In May the first version of *Sanctuary* (novel) is completed and is immediately rejected by his publisher as too scandalous. In June, although both families oppose the marriage because of Faulkner's uncertain economic prospects, he and Estelle are married. She already has two children; they will have two more, one of whom dies in infancy. The marriage begins disastrously, with Estelle attempting suicide. *The Sound and the Fury* (novel), published 7 October, is a critical success but earns little. Wall Street crashes 24 October, spreading economic panic and ruin contributing to the Great Depression, which will last until 1942. While working nights at the university power plant, Faulkner begins *As I Lay Dying* on 25 October; writing under economic pressure, he finishes the manuscript on 11 December and the typescript a month later. |
| 1930 | *As I Lay Dying* published by Cape and Smith, New York. It gives Faulkner's fictional county the name *Yoknapatawpha.* |
| 1931 | Revised version of *Sanctuary* (novel) and *These 13* (stories) published. In New York Faulkner is briefly lionized and meets several other writers. For almost two decades, however, Faulkner's repute in France will for the most part exceed his recognition in the United States. |
| 1932–1953 | Writes intermittently for the movies, usually working in Hollywood for several weeks or months at a time; |

making significant contributions to several films, including *To Have and to Have Not* (based on Hemingway's novel) and *The Big Sleep* (based on Raymond Chandler's novel). Also sells several of his own stories and novels to film studios.

1932    Publication of *Light in August* (novel).

1933    Publication of *A Green Bough* (poems).

1934    Publication of *Dr. Martino and Other Stories*.

1935    Publication of *Pylon* (novel). Begins liaison with Meta Doherty Carpenter in Hollywood. In later years has liaisons with Joan Williams and Jean Stein.

1936    Publication of *Absalom, Absalom!* (novel)

1938    Publication of *The Unvanquished* (novel).

1939    Portents of future recognition: elected to the National Institute of Arts and Letters and made the subject of admiring essays by George Marion O'Donnell and Conrad Aiken as well as a *Time* cover story. Publication of *The Wild Palms* (a hybrid: a novel made up of two alternating stories). Faulkner offers the manuscript of *Absalom, Absalom!* to the cause of the Loyalists in the Spanish Civil War.

1940    Publication of *The Hamlet*, the first novel of the Snopes trilogy.

1942    Publication of *Go Down, Moses and Other Stories* (another hybrid of stories and novel; later published simply as *Go Down, Moses*).

1946    Publication of *The Portable Faulkner*, edited by Malcolm Cowley. Except for *Sanctuary*, Faulkner's novels are out of print and his reputation is at an ebb; this anthology helps to turn the tide.

1948    Publication of *Intruder in the Dust* (novel). Elected to American Academy of Arts and Letters.

1949    Publication of *Knight's Gambit* (stories).

| | |
|---|---|
| 1950 | Wins the Nobel Prize for Literature for the previous year. Receives American Academy's Howells Medal for Fiction. *Collected Stories* published and awarded National Book Award for Fiction. |
| 1951 | *Requiem for a Nun* (novel) published; later produced as a play in French (by Albert Camus) and American versions. France awards him Legion of Honor. |
| 1952–1962 | Now writes explicitly and speaks publicly on politics, especially on racial issues. During the desegregation movement, his attacks on racism and segregation win him admiration as well as denunciation (including that of family members), either for attacking racism or for advocating a gradualist approach to desegregation. Also travels extensively as cultural ambassador for the State Department. |
| 1954 | *A Fable* (novel) published; awarded Pulitzer Prize and National Book Award. |
| 1955 | *Big Woods* (stories) published. |
| 1957 | *The Town* published, the second novel in the Snopes trilogy. Writer-in-residence at University of Virginia; alternates between residence in Virginia and Mississippi until his death. Receives Silver Medal of Greek Academy. |
| 1959 | Publication of the last novel in the Snopes trilogy, *The Mansion.* |
| 1962 | Publication of *The Reivers* (novel). Suffers the last of a series of bad falls from horses. Dies of a heart attack a few weeks later on 6 July, the birthday of his great-grandfather. |

# Literary and
# Historical Context

❡

The old Yocona River bridge. Photograph courtesy Yoknapatawpha Press.

# 1

## Cultural Stories:
## The Roaring Twenties, the Great Depression,
## and the Rise of the "Rednecks"

William Faulkner perhaps wanted public recognition more than anything else. He thought of this recognition as a "No to death," a kind of immortality in the minds of readers to come. In fall and winter of 1929–30 he had just married a woman with two children from a previous marriage and was planning to buy a run-down antebellum mansion, all without having yet earned a living from his writing. So his need for recognition was also immediately, almost desperately, practical.[1]

As I Lay Dying was written at this time when personal economic and artistic crisis was worsened by national disaster. Psychologically considered, its coolly crafted nightmare vision seems designed to provide Faulkner mental control over fear that he would fail to win public recognition and literary immortality. This artistically controlled nightmare is the horrible-humorous pageant in which Addie Bundren's stinking coffin is grotesquely exhibited to the public, as if in a parody of recognition after death.

Socially considered, the novel simultaneously represents a nightmare journey in which a family's cooperation grows shakily from their mixed private motives and illustrates the economic blindness of their society. As I Lay Dying speaks to social issues pressing on Faulkner that were inseparable from his artistic hopes and family situation. These issues, centering on cooperation versus individualism, extend before and after the time the novel was written. But cooperation and an individualism of a certain kind are the stuff of different cultural stories—different shared narratives by which (usually unconsciously) people live their lives. In 1929–30 these cultural stories collided head-on.

Faulkner started writing *As I Lay Dying* on Friday, 25 October 1929, while he supervised the night shift at the University of Mississippi power plant. At this moment a larger story was breaking, as newspapers reported that on the previous day, to be known as "Black Thursday," there had occurred the greatest crash in the history of Wall Street up to that time. The previous cultural story, entitled "The Roaring Twenties," began to disappear from the papers. In all but name the next cultural story, to be called "The Thirties" or "The Great Depression," had begun. It buried "The Twenties," at least as much as any decade's story can obliterate another's, since much that the twenties represented wasn't really dead but only somewhat in remission, and this decade has remained an important image in American life. So has its opposing story, "The Thirties," which brought to the forefront problems and opportunities preceding that decade and continuing today.

One of the conventions of cultural and other stories, however, is to give decades and Thursdays, like everything else, simplifying metaphorical names, to make certain distinctive features stand out dramatically. In a similar partly literal and partly metaphorical sense, *As I Lay Dying* was the last major American novel written in the twenties and the first major American novel published in the thirties.

"Rugged individualism" had been the watchword of the twenties' boom years. According to the story this decade told itself, the ideal was the risk-taking entrepreneur or business, free to pursue profit and ruggedly dare or suffer the risks of failure with no "outside interference" of regulation or an economic safety net. On the personal side, the ideal meant looking out for oneself generally in a demanding, competitive world and translated easily into an energetic pursuit of individual pleasure, as reflected in the decade's self-created reputation as the wild jazz age.

Under this doctrine of competitive individualism, both business and pleasure roared—or appeared to, since by the late twenties severe problems in farming and industry had begun to surface. After the 1929 crash, when this doctrine was applied to restrict international trade in the Hawley-Smoot Tariff Act, the last piece was in place for the economic debacle and political crisis that followed.

In the sphere of "high" literature, embedded uneasily in twenties culture, a marked interest in examining the individual psyche fit the mood of the dominant cultural story. But this embedded story of individualism both opposed the explicit politico-economic form of individualism in some ways and repeated it in others.

Twenties stories of the "lost generation," like F. Scott Fitzgerald's *This Side of Paradise* and *The Beautiful and Damned* and Ernest Hemingway's *The Sun Also Rises* and *A Farewell to Arms*, portrayed lost individuals. They had lost community, a sense that they belonged to a continuing collective life. Loneliness, disillusionment and anger with the conventions of belief and behavior of previous generations, and the related near impossibility of communication—these were the accounts of post–World War I life that this literature gave directly or indirectly, and Faulkner's twenties novels partly bespoke this alienation.

Faulkner's work took its bearings from older writers such as Joseph Conrad, whose *The Nigger of the "Narcissus,"* which tells of a dying black man's power over a ship's crew, helped inspire *As I Lay Dying*. Another influential older writer was Sherwood Anderson, whose literary example in novels like *Winesburg, Ohio* as well as tall-tale swapping with Faulkner in New Orleans provided additional inspiration for representing the Bundrens' milieu by combining realism and surrealism. So did James Joyce's famous innovations in the interior monologues of the epic comedy *Ulysses*, which Faulkner had also recently drawn on in his brilliant novel, *The Sound and the Fury*. And over all these influences towered that of T. S. Eliot's poetry of isolated, uprooted individuals, particularly in *The Waste Land*.

Sometimes, as in Hemingway, there was a last-ditch "lost generation" ideal corresponding to "ruggedness." It was a stoic ability to endure a world of lost individuals, living without the "outside" regulation or safety net of community. This endurance was anchored in a distrust of language and an emphasis on basic physical activity, perhaps shared with a few others. At one level, this "twenties" combination of traits describes Addie Bundren, as a female Southern second cousin to the Hemingway hero. But *As I Lay Dying* sets her within another story, a "thirties" narrative of difficult cooperative action amid economic hardship. This narrative foreshadows much thirties writing, most obviously the story of a poor family's epic journey that John Steinbeck's *The Grapes of Wrath* would tell in 1939.

*As I Lay Dying* in fact foreshadows a decade-long national attempt to breathe life back into cooperative action in order to deal with the economic ruin that to some appeared to foretell the end of the nation. Steinbeck much more explicitly than Faulkner depicted a family's struggle to move beyond both individualist outlook and blood ties toward a larger communal belonging, expressed in organized collective action against oppression. The immense success of *The Grapes of Wrath* suggests that, as part of the new cultural story, it served as welcome therapy, helping Americans to manage, if not cure, their ambivalence between lingering competitive individualism and desired cooperation against social injustice. Thirties laws establishing Social Security, creating jobs, regulating business and investment, affirming the right to collective bargaining, and protecting the right to strike told the same corrective story.

In the South, a whole region was still trying to recover from the devastation of the previous immense threat to the nation, the Civil War, and from the economic colonization of the South by the North that followed. In that war, it was evident that Southern politics, like the states' rights doctrine, and the Southern cultural habit of touchy individual independence reinforced each other. Whether we call this mutual reinforcement cultural politics or political culture, it was the South's own long-standing version of rugged individualism. What Faulkner knew to his bones is that, particularly in the South, the family is a potent incubator of this cultural story.

The twenties never did roar very much in the South, and the decade sputtered badly for Southern farmers, who were already in a long-term depression. When the national Great Depression awoke many Americans to the need for greater cooperation, the South had been both advocating and struggling with its own forms of collective action for some time.

Cooperative action in various forms was urged nearly across the political spectrum in the thirties, but nationally, "collectivism" was the slogan especially of the political Left. Comparably, for several decades populist and progressive movements in the South had fought to improve the economic and political conditions of disadvantaged groups, especially poor white farmers, by banding them together against wealthy planters and their business and banking allies. Faulkner's family had participated energetically, though ambivalently, in these politics, allying with a leader of the "revolt of the rednecks," James K. Vardaman.

Nevertheless, despite (or because of) this populism, for the South the story of the collective had a particular conservatism. Traditionally, the Southern collective ideal meant a respect for the long-standing bonds and mores of community. It meant traditional social hierarchies embodied in ceremonious politeness. If these folkways were honored at least in forms and appearance, then the individual—especially the white male, and especially the husband and father—was supposed to be free to mind his own business without others' interference.

This rule of conservative noninterference applied at all levels. After the heyday of progressivism (1900–1920), the collective story of white people increasingly came again to take one form, as it had in the nineteenth century: protecting our way of life from outside (read "Northern") interference. Primarily, though not exclusively, "our way of life" was a code phrase for white cooperation in a presumed supremacy over black people. Because whites widely believed this cultural story of race superiority, even when the populist movement directed attention to class injustice it usually did so at the cost of a poisonous racism that blocked cooperation between poor white and black farmers, and collective action was often diverted into keeping blacks in a socially debased position.

Given the potency of these already existing, conflicting cultural stories of individualism and collectivism in his local society and his family, Faulkner didn't need to be clairvoyant to write his novel of transition, *As I Lay Dying*. It is a tightrope walk in several senses. First of all, it moves between "twenties/Southern individualism" and "thirties/Southern collectivism," each honeycombed with ambivalences and cross-purposes. Here the novel foreshadows the national attempt to regain balance after the excesses of the decade that ended as Faulkner, under economic pressure and working in a power plant, began to write about the impoverished Bundrens.

While accompanying his uncle on his political campaigns into the country and small towns, Faulkner had discovered the seeds of his major treatments of the rural lower class, which he first compared and contrasted with the untamable power of the escaping "spotted horses" that he had seen in a hamlet in 1922. (Their literary descendant is Jewel Bundren's barely tamed horse.) From this "spotted horses" material—which he titles, among other things, "Father Abraham" and "As I Lay Dying"—Faulkner develops two main fictions. Quite characteristically, from the same source he conceives fictions that are foils and complements for each other, though their decade-long separation in publication makes this hard to see.

One fiction, foreseen early in the "spotted horse" material, centers on the Snopes family and its rise in society through the sharp economic and political practices of the clan leader, Flem. (Flem is mentioned in *As I Lay Dying*, and a nephew Snopes appears offstage as a slick horse trader, but the family's chronicle is primarily the Snopes trilogy, which begins to appear 10 years later in *The Hamlet.*) The other fiction centers on the Bundren family and its social inertia, also created by economic practices with political implications and epitomized in its "clan leader," Anse. Faulkner's fifth published novel, *As I Lay Dying* is the third published installment developing his principal fictional society, and it baptizes this society with the old Indian name for the flooded river the Bundrens cross: Yoknapatawpha. (Actually it's easy to pronounce: YOK-na-pa-TAW-pha—meaning, Faulkner said, "Water runs slow over flat land.")[2]

# 2

# Stories out of Stories I:
# The Novel's Impact

*As I Lay Dying* is a key text in the writings of a novelist who has received world acclaim. Because of the bold, memorable clarity of the novel's central action and image—the burial journey—and because of its combination of straightforward realist narrative with a variety of nonrealist techniques, *As I Lay Dying* offers a rather accessible entry into Faulkner's more challenging major writings. Indeed, more than most writers, Faulkner benefits from being read as the producer of a *body* of work. Admirers of Faulkner may have their favorite one or two books, but there is general agreement that what is most impressive is the accumulating force of reading the acknowledged major fictions: the novels *The Sound and the Fury*, *As I Lay Dying*, *Light in August*, *Absalom, Absalom!*, *The Hamlet*, *Go Down, Moses*, and the short stories "A Rose for Emily," "That Evening Sun," "Red Leaves," and "Barn Burning."

To put the matter another way, *As I Lay Dying* is important because it contributes substantially to the development of, and our introduction to, Faulkner's influential fictional world, the society this novel names "Yoknapatawpha." This making of a whole fictive society is often used as a criterion of literary importance. Readers have found Faulkner outstanding for the ethical, historical, and artistic density of his fictional universe.

What's more, they have found that *As I Lay Dying* beckons them through and beyond the society of Yoknapatawpha to a durably provocative vision of what it means to be a human being or to exist in our society. In evoking this vision, Addie's family-borne coffin can mark the memory like Hester Prynne's scarlet letter or Huck Finn's raft.

As suggested in the preceding chapter, the novel raises issues specific to Southern life that were reinforced by the national crisis as the twenties passed into the thirties. But as with many valuable books, this novel has, if anything, increased its power to both illuminate a particular time and place and suggest powerful analogies to continuing potentials and problems in our lives within modern societies. One reason for its enduring—even increasing—power is that by concentrating on the intermediate social level of the family, it intensely focuses relations between individuals in light of broader social relations.

Part of the novel's effect involves the weightiness Faulkner locates in the thoughts and passions of his farm working-class characters. Before *As I Lay Dying*, Faulkner's novels had concentrated on middle-class and upper-class people and had used sturdy, hard-working farmers—the MacCallums in *Sartoris/Flags in the Dust*—as a foil for the confused but apparently more complex and fine-strung psyches of the upper classes. Now, Faulkner concentrates on the lower economic class and doesn't limit us to an exterior view of the characters, restricted by their rural speech to apparently simple thoughts and feelings. He renders their dialect wonderfully, but he also doesn't hesitate to frame their interior monologues, soliloquies, and actions in the most sophisticated language and allusiveness—beginning with the reference to Homer's *Odyssey* in the title, to be discussed later.

Readers have found the novel important, then, because of its use of enlarging frames: if the Bundrens think tortured thoughts and do bizarre things, these are part and parcel of Yoknapatawpha society at every social level and of the larger-than-life universe of epic, tragedy, myth, and frontier tall tale. Like Melville's *Moby-Dick* and Joyce's *Ulysses*, Faulkner's novel thus offers a corrective to a superficial, flattened view of poor or "common" people. However, while giving its characters considerable empathy in these ways and others, the novel still maintains a critical distance that also helps to correct such reductive sentimental clichés as "the plight of the

Southern farmer" and to spotlight the characters' complicity in social blindness.

If we consider this novel's importance in the art of narrative, it significantly carries forward Faulkner's innovations with narrative techniques strikingly developed in his previous published novel, *The Sound and the Fury*. These are experiments in making narrative technique contribute heavily to the story. For example, the disruption of conventional assumptions about narrative in *As I Lay Dying*, such as the mixture of rural dialect and sophisticated language in the Bundrens' mind-voice, is keyed to the novel's critique of specific social conventions. Because it ranges so widely across the spectrum of realist and nonrealist techniques, this novel has been recognized as a reference book of the novelist's art.

Yet with all this technical diversity, many readers find in *As I Lay Dying* something distinctively "Faulknerian" that we can call by such names as the writer's voice, sensibility, or novelistic intelligence. In modern Western culture, this distinctive mark of the maker—a characteristic, stirring interaction with the world and with writing—is a mark of literary importance (though contemporary literary criticism has challenged this priority given to the author). Few readers can mistake the Faulknerian voice, which they usually associate with ornate rhetoric, though this novel shows him to be adept at a number of styles, from spare to florid.

For all these reasons manifested in *As I Lay Dying*, Faulkner has always been a writer's writer. Even when he doesn't specifically influence a writer's themes or styles, his constant pushing at the limits of fiction's subject matter and form continues to excite other writers and artists by expanding their sense of what a novel could be or what one might dare in any genre or medium. The work of a contemporary Latin American "magical realist," the Nobel Prize winner Gabriel García Márquez, exemplifies in both subject and form the impact of Faulkner—in particular, how *As I Lay Dying* provides inspirations for him as a social-minded magical realist. Writers who are influenced by García Márquez also indirectly feel and in turn transmit something of Faulkner's impact even if they have never encountered his work directly. Such prolific breeding of stories from other stories is a recurring theme of Faulkner's writing in general and of this novel in particular.

Perhaps what keeps bringing many readers back to *As I Lay Dying*, as to the rest of Faulkner's work, is suggested in his praise of Albert Camus as a writer who constantly searched and questioned himself. The questioning, exploratory intelligence in Faulkner makes for a ferment of revisionary activity.[3] Discontented not only with clichés and conventions, it critiques many of Faulkner's own deepest impulses and opens his writer's voice to alternative voices both within and without himself. *As I Lay Dying* communicates this audible energy of exploration. Take, for example, two features just noted: his revisionary treatment of poor white farmers (from the MacCallums of *Sartoris* to the Bundrens of this novel), and the multiplicity of voices that drive the narrative (not only multiple levels of colloquial and formal literary language but numerous narrators as well). Or consider the changing perspectives on Cash, showing in him first a rather cloddish literal-mindedness and then more and more an insightful, although limited, moral capacity. Or, most dramatically, the sudden reappearance of Addie in the novel, revolutionizing our view of her because we have assumed that since she is dead she is beyond giving us a new interior perspective. Faulkner works with language and form to embody and interrogate the novel's themes and to involve us in acting out this process as we read.

Faulkner's habit of revisionary questioning led him over his career to revise remarkably the fairly standard prejudices about region, class, race, and gender common to one of his generation and circumstances, although imprints of one's time and place are finally ineradicable and in his case enter complexly into his interest as a writer. Yet, as I have also suggested, *As I Lay Dying* probes to the limits of this very independent-mindedness when it takes the form of a certain kind of individualism. From this standpoint, whether we agree with this or that position we infer from Faulkner's writing is less important than his valuable example of revisionary questioning and self-critique.

*As I Lay Dying*, as a revisionary novel on a tightrope between crucial American decades, is shaped by a wealth of literary and broad cultural stories. Because Faulkner's direct and indirect influence on culture-makers in literature and other media has been so pervasive, his novelistic sensibility has in turn helped to shape the sensibilities that shape ours. Especially for academically trained readers, this novel has helped to form the very criteria and tastes by which we judge this novel important. But whether or not we have read *As I Lay Dying* or Faulkner's other writings, their wide diffusion in "high" and popular culture has helped to furnish our minds with images, characters, feelings, and ideas. This novel is important, then, because in reading it we can engage its influential self-questioning more directly with our own questions and answers.

# 3

## Stories out of Stories II:
## The Critics Comment

Critical reception involves the recognition that a writer receives from the public and even from himself. If Faulkner wanted recognition more than anything else in life, he also wanted it on terms that he himself could recognize and respect.

*As I Lay Dying* was written under conditions that gave Faulkner a large incentive for such stock-taking, and his changing assessment of it is geared to this fact. Critics today agree that a writer's commentary about his or her work has to take its chances along with everyone else's, but it can help reveal the writer's intentions at the time of writing or later values at the time of commentary (whether these are actually achieved in the text has to be put to the test of analysis). As we noted in chapter 1, at the time he wrote the novel, 1929–30, Faulkner was in an economic and artistic crisis aggravated by national disaster. As shown in both families' opposition to his new marriage, many around him disbelieved that he could have a professional writing career because the sales of his previous work had been so disappointing.

In the spirit of the risk-taking twenties, Faulkner gambled on a twofold strategy in which, to oversimplify a bit, he wrote *Sanctuary* to make money from the general public and *As I Lay Dying* to make a reputation among connoisseurs. Actually, the first novel was immediately turned down by his publisher, and Faulkner had to write the second while working at night in a power plant. Faulkner soon revised *Sanctuary* (at his own expense, when he could ill afford it) to bring it up to his artistic standards, but its horrific rape and lurid brothel and gangster scenes were admittedly designed to make money—and would do so in 1932, when he sold the movie rights and also won a job in Hollywood writing movies. The second novel, begun after *Sanctuary*'s initial rejection in the summer of 1929, is also written so as to be generally accessible, though it is artistically elaborate.

Given his previous lack of success and the need to support his new family, Faulkner appears to have written *As I Lay Dying* while entertaining the thought that it might be either his last book or a new beginning for his professional career. As he began in October, he faced a contract that required him to complete a novel by March. As Dianne Luce has noted, he was determined to prove that he was a professional who could deliver a fine job under a deadline. He said he wanted to write "a book by which, at a pinch, I can stand or fall if I never touch ink again." *The Sound and the Fury*, just published, had described a preacher demonstrating the virtuosity of his powerful speaking voice as being like a man on a tightrope. *As I Lay Dying*, a similar risky feat of skill, is like a tightrope walk determining whether Faulkner will stand or fall, and it's as if he enacts these possibilities in the novel's images of balancing, falling, and recovery as well as its ambivalence about individual risk.[4]

For several years, after this novel in combination with *Sanctuary* had seen him through his first great crisis of confidence and income, he called *As I Lay Dying* his best novel. Later he would consistently claim his best to be the preceding work, *The Sound and the Fury*, for the paradoxical reason that in it, he felt, he had tried to do the most and so had had his most "splendid failure." The second judgment is consistent with Faulkner's habitual self-challenging, but he could talk this way, it should also be noted, after he had received recognition and financial security in the last decade or so of his life. When such success was still far from certain in his younger days, he preferred his achieved exhibition of skill in *As I Lay Dying*.

He always referred to this novel as an exhibition of skill or feat of strength by using the term *tour de force*. At first, this term conveyed his pride at his ability, under pressure, to show his diverse mastery of the writer's craft, when it was vital for him to do so. Later, when he had written several other powerful novels and the memory of his successful gamble under pressure apparently had faded, he announced that his highest standard was attempting the impossible. When he spoke of the novel at this later time, the other side of the ambiguous term *tour de force* came to the fore: a mere display of adroitness or ingenuity, which he later said had been too easy for him.

In contrast to the exhilarating sense of discovery he said he had felt writing the first section of *The Sound and the Fury*, when he found out what he would say as he wrote it, he stressed the calculated deliberateness of *As I Lay Dying*, which he claimed to have written in six weeks without changing a word. Faulkner exaggerates here: although the manuscript was done in a little over six weeks, he revised it significantly and carefully it revised again in about four weeks of typing. Nevertheless, what is most important is that the process and energy of "re-vision," as noted before, is exactly what the book displays, along with his desire to convey a sense of masterful control over his exploratory improvisations.

Faulkner's devotion to drawing out his reader's own supple revisionary outlook through all available means in *As I Lay Dying* has meant that the book from the first has attracted an extraordinary range of commentary. The novel has proved elusive because its revisionary shifts in perspective combine tragedy with humor; bold, outrageous subject matter and images with delicate indirection; and conservative with populist sympathies.

Faulkner himself objected to early critical discussions of "the sociological picture" supposedly presented in *As I Lay Dying* and his other works.[5] Faulkner's objection is valid, many contemporary critics feel, in the sense that it opposes too-literal interpretations that assume that literature simply copies naked reality, as if—to exaggerate these interpretations a little—his characters were sociological lab specimens demonstrating weird burial customs among poor Mississippi farmers. Nevertheless, these critics would agree that while Faulkner is indeed sociological in his insights, he works as a *novelist*, using fictional devices such as heightening and distortion in order, for example, to expose the social distortions that custom obscures. In general, however, over the decades critics have divided over not only what it means to be a "sociological" writer but what it means to be a novelist, and this novel has provided a test case for this division, just as it was a test case for Faulkner's continuation in his career.

In 1933, in fact, Faulkner commented that Southern writers tried "to draw a savage indictment of the contemporary scene" or "to escape from it into a makebelieve region" of the romanticized Southern past, and he had done both up to that point.[6] How much escapism there is even in early Faulkner novels like *Sartoris* has been disputed, and critics have long recognized the indictment of modern society embodied in *Sanctuary*, but they are only now developing a strong sense of how *Sanctuary*'s companion novel, *As I Lay Dying*, similarly arraigns its times.

Although early commentators on the novel had difficulty recognizing the indictment as such, its cold fury outraged some of them and disturbed most. In general they acknowledged Faulkner's talent, but as with his earlier novels several critics saw a troublesome mismatch between superior talent and inferior subject matter, or else evidence of morbidity and "the cult of cruelty."

Even sociologically committed critics of the Left took this novel and Faulkner's other thirties writings sharply to task for lacking a constructive viewpoint. Seeking open polemics that could fire immediate social action to meet the emergency of the Depression, these critics had little taste for the indirect persuasions of the dialogues among Faulkner's multiple voices. Left criticism echoed traditional humanism in deploring Faulkner's apparent indulgence in morbidity, horror, and violence featuring "abnormal" and "unrepresentative" characters. A British critic contrasted Faulkner unfavorably with Erskine Caldwell (whose novels of poor whites, such as *Tobacco Road*, Faulkner in fact anticipated) because Caldwell explicitly recommended collective farming. On the other hand, the reviewer for the Manchester *Guardian* admired Faulkner's study of "peasant character."

On the whole, however, the American reviews were favorable, much more favorable than the British. Laudatory reviews recommended *As I Lay Dying* as an artistically forceful rendering of life despite its potential for scandalizing squeamish readers. They disagreed about what kind of rendering this was—tragic, comic, or ironic—and thus inaugurated a discussion continuing to the present. Disagreement about the novel's tone was especially strong in the fifties, when critics described the novel as Faulkner's most kindly and genial as well as his bitterest. Further, the favorable reviewers' emphasis on artistic treatment over subject matter became a strong theme for the academic criticism that began after Faulkner won the 1949 Nobel Prize for literature.

Foreshadowing that recognition was the respect Faulkner had obtained from his fellow writers by 1930, particularly from writers and critics in France, where in 1934 *As I Lay Dying* became the second of his novels to be published in translation. As France went through the hard times of the thirties and then defeat and occupation in World War II, French intellectuals saw in Faulkner's representation of his fictional South a bracing artistic resourcefulness in the face of defeat. Nevertheless, by the time Malcolm Cowley published his anthology, *The Portable Faulkner* (1946), *As I Lay Dying*—like every other Faulkner book except *Sanctuary*—was out of print, and Faulkner was trapped in a low-paying contract in Hollywood.

Cowley's anthology of selections from Faulkner's writings helped to turn the tide by suggesting that individual works like *As I Lay Dying* had to be read in the context of Faulkner's whole fictional world, Yoknapatawpha. Faulkner, Cowley wrote in an introduction that reversed his censure of Faulkner in the thirties, was the creator of a major explanatory myth of the South. Robert Penn Warren seconded and extended this view by asserting that this myth of the South resounded with universal themes. Faulkner, critics came to agree, wrote not simply about Southerners but about the modern world and the human condition. This view opposed the notion that Faulkner was merely a narrow regionalist, and it fit the general critical emphasis on universality accompanying America's dramatic rise to world power during and after the war. The focus on "myth" in one sense or another—and, even more, the emphasis on the related idea of universality—also became a dominant part of the academic criticism of Faulkner and his fifth novel, either alone or in combination with an analysis of Faulkner's artistic formalism.

The socially oriented studies of Faulkner could find comfort in several Faulknerian statements like the one already quoted about indicting society. The formalist approaches could find comfort in Faulknerian assertions, scattered throughout his career, that he was primarily a storyteller, one whose art per se takes precedence over all other elements. Universalist interpretations could find comfort in some of his statements in the forties and in his Nobel Prize speech, where he said that writers like himself wished to remind people of "old universal truths," such as love and honor and pity, and so help human beings to "endure and prevail" (Meriwether, 120).

The best illustration of the universalist approach, one that wishes to subsume the other two, is found in the work of critic Cleanth Brooks. He saw in *As I Lay Dying* an exemplary text for his position. In his influential studies of Faulkner, especially his 1963 book, *William Faulkner: The Yoknapatawpha Country*, Brooks stressed that Faulkner's novel is not "sociological"—not, that is, a literal study of deprived, depraved rustics who supposedly populate Mississippi. Rather, it analyzes the nature of the heroic act, performed by various universal types of human being. Yet in his book as a whole Brooks also acknowledges extensively what other critics might call Faulkner's "sociology" with general background discussions of Southern life. In general, though not specifically with regard to *As I Lay Dying*, he emphasizes that Faulkner does indeed indict modern society from the vantage of a more simplified, nonmetropolitan fictional world. However, Brooks believes, Faulkner does so "universally" because in essential ways modern life violates timeless, universal principles.

Partly because this thesis permitted Brooks to deal flexibly with diverse matters relevant to many approaches, reading his 1963 book soon became a rite of passage for students of Faulkner, and much discussion of *As I Lay Dying* and Faulkner in general continues to be indebted to this critic or argues directly or indirectly with his position.

Other critics, like Richard P. Adams, similarly found that the meaning and power of *As I Lay Dying* lie in its evocation not of culturally specific stories but of universal ones, myths of ancient Greece and elsewhere having to do with death and rebirth. These interpretations typically rely on the novel's debt to T. S. Eliot's *The Waste Land* and Faulkner's reading of Sir James Frazer's study of myth. Comparably, with significant exceptions, studies of the novel's use of Christian symbolism and doctrine have often reinforced a universalist interpretation. This approach to the novel through universalist sacred stories was particularly prevalent in the fifties and sixties. But whereas the mythical approach tends to be optimistic—stressing the triumph of life over death—another form of universalist approach prevalent in those decades—the "existentialist" interpretation—finds in the novel a depiction of humankind's grimly absurd fate. Although some discussions simplistically equate existentialism with nihilism, Calvin Bedient avoids this pitfall in drawing on existentialism for his analysis of the characters as isolated makers of meaning.

Themes that critics have highlighted include, besides the nature of heroism, the nature of time or being, isolation, dehumanized humanity, and language. Until recently, critics since the fifties have for the most part treated such themes in a universalist framework, without much concern for what they might mean as specifically cultural preoccupations.

Studies of the novel's remarkable innovations in style and form have been as numerous as might be expected. The narrative form has been described as an attempt to transcend language, in keeping with Addie's criticism of words and Faulkner's view of poetry. It has also been analyzed as a failure, because of either temporal inconsistencies (e.g., the narrative shifts in verb tense) or a conflict between plot and consciousness. In general, however, Faulkner's innovations have been explained as modernist representations of the dynamic nature of individual consciousness or the flux of reality. Here critics like Stephen Ross have found affinities or influences especially in the philosophy of Henri Bergson, with his description of fluid time as it is experienced in consciousness; other critics, such as Watson Branch, have found analogies in modern art, especially cubism.

Given a general interest in psychological interpretation and the variety of characters in such a short novel, studies of character have been even more numerous than studies of form and style, although the two have usually been related since Olga Vickery's ground-breaking studies concentrating on Addie and her effect on her children. Like Brooks's work, Vickery's has been prominent in critical debates, but its lack of interest in the social dimension beyond this individual-family relationship is even more characteristic of most approaches to this novel. Her view that the novel's ethical center is Cash, because he supposedly matures morally and intellectually, has been challenged to many critics' satisfaction. But her shrewd comments on psychology, form, and theme have done much to advance the discussion of the novel. More often than Cash, Addie and Darl have been proposed as the focus of the writer's sympathies and values, though other critics explicitly or implicitly deny that any single character has this standing. If later discussions of whatever persuasion have been able to take up other topics, it was because they have been building on such foundational studies of character and theme—including early essays establishing, for example, that Vardaman is not, as some had thought, retarded but is instead a traumatized young child.

André Bleikasten's extensively admired book-length study of the novel in 1973 incorporated and expanded much of the most valuable existing criticism to interpret the novel as a rendition of the "scandalous" finite limitations of human existence, in the face of which Faulkner wagers his universe of words.

Most recently, as in our present discussion of *As I Lay Dying*, criticism has begun to return to a social perspective on the novel, after a long period of neglect. This contemporary approach differs from earlier social and historical studies in that it is informed by recent theories of society and language. These theories draw certain conclusions from the widely held premise that neither the writer nor anyone else has direct access to a naked reality. A primary conclusion is that reality comes to us preinterpreted and prepackaged by our society's communication in all its forms—its discourse—which is everything from casual conversation to scientific and mathematical symbolic ordering. To write a novel is to confront not an unadorned reality to depict but some portion of this discourse of reality to take part in. Another conclusion is that, whatever the possibility of universal claims, as with Anse's claim to act only for sacred reasons, they often conceal powerful self-interest. (So, for example, our social approach here views *As I Lay Dying* as participating in specific large networks of informal and formal stories about reality that shape people's lives and represent conflicting social interests.) The social approach, then, tends to focus on how novels work in our lives in specific times and places.

In the specific time and place of reading, each reader's reception of the novel, however much or little stimulated and enlightened by others' reactions, takes its distinctive part. In the last chapter, we will return to consider what that part may be.

# A Reading

¶

Yocona (locally pronounced "Yocknee") River in flood, like its fictional counterpart in *As I Lay Dying.* Photograph courtesy Yoknapatawpha Press.

# 4

# *What Kind of Book Is This?:*
# *Outrage and Family Secrets*

## OUTRAGE: BETWEEN PRIVATE AND PUBLIC, HUMOR AND TRAGEDY

"It's a outrage," Rachel Samson cries out at one point in the Bundrens' burial journey, and later Lula Armstid exactly echoes Rachel's comical grammar and sincere sense of grievance.[7] It's a succinct phrase that bears repeating. These women could be talking about the book itself: "a outrage," grievous and yet humorous, humorous yet grievous, in an unstable mixture that is itself potentially outrageous to its readers. A comment of Faulkner's seems as tailor-made to this novel as Cash's coffin is to Addie: "There's not too fine a distinction between humor and tragedy . . . even tragedy is in a way walking a tightrope between . . . the bizarre and the terrible" (Gwynn and Blotner, 39). Seldom if ever has a novel combined so simple a basic action—death and burial—with such outrageousness, part of which is the complex way the simple action is told. The women protest a similar apparently perverse complication of a simple act of burial into a bizarre and terrible spectacle.

Rachel and Lula deplore Anse Bundren's unwillingness to give his wife Addie an immediate burial. Instead, Anse persists through formidable obstacles and delays in carrying her decaying corpse in the heat of a Mississippi July to the distant cemetery in Jefferson, where he has promised to bury her and where she is finally interred nine days after her death. Although he acts in the name of this promise to his wife that he calls sacred (*AILD*, 126), to Rachel and Lula his failure to give the hideously smelling corpse a quick, decent burial really makes a mockery of his promise. To them, his action, instead of being sacred, offends against one of the most sacred proprieties of society, the proper treatment of the dead.

Anse is far from alone in outrageously flouting conventional behavior. As the astonished and indignant black man exclaims when the Bundrens pass him on the outskirts of Jefferson, "Great God . . . what they got in that wagon?" (*AILD*, 212). What is disconcerting is not only what Anse has, but what they all have in that wagon, an outrageous load besides the corpse. Tull says something of Anse (*AILD*, 66) that is first of all true of his whole family, with its punning name: the *burden* the Bundrens carry is, most of all, themselves. By the time the wagon reaches Jefferson, the novel has given us reason to understand that "they" can refer to more than even Anse's "poor white" family. The family's determination to carry out a journey that is both a strange transgression and a sacred mission casts an eerie light on a larger stubborn persistence: an ongoing society that is also its own burden—part of which, the novel hints, is its notion of the sacred.

A whole society acts in (willing or unwilling) collaboration to help carry its very own Bundrens to their destination and thus in effect to flout itself. The novel offers another fine, broadly applicable phrase in describing Addie's body being taken to the wagon. At first her body seems, in modesty, to resist being carried out into the open, but then suddenly it seems to will the opposite: "a passionate reversal that flouts its own desire and need" (*AILD*, 87). Such passionate reversal is the basis of this novel. Desires and needs flout themselves, and such self-flouting becomes itself a desire and need.

A common approach to *As I Lay Dying* explains the Bundrens' behavior as the result of the individual psychologies of the family members. Conveniently, the back cover of the Vintage Books paperback edition cited here exemplifies this way of understanding the book: "[as the Bundrens and others tell the story] they reveal what Addie calls their own 'secret and selfish thought' [*AILD*, 153]—their *private responses* to Addie's life and their own *separate reasons* for undertaking the perilous journey to bury her" (italics added). We can readily agree that, although *As I Lay Dying* offers plenty of action and conversation, to a remarkable extent the life in this novel is life lived in the head. Understanding the Bundrens' motives in all their privacy is certainly important, as the novel sifts them out from various psychological layers (for example, in many of the italicized passages). But commentators also often note that the Bundrens' motives as well as their entire personalities depend on each other, so we overlook far too much if we think about their reasons as simply separate. For example, many readers have noticed how the different attitudes Addie has toward each of her children affect their identities, as these are revealed in turn in their private and not-so-private attitudes toward her death and her burial journey. This shaping influence suggests that the Bundrens' private "secret and selfish thought[s]" are important not by themselves but in relation to something else—the Bundren identity as a group.

After all, there are families in which a daughter, like Dewey Dell, would not have to be so secretive about her pregnancy; but Dewey Dell is so passionately secretive that, because her brother Darl has intuited her condition, she imagines stabbing him to death (*AILD*, 107) and later instigates his commitment to the asylum at Jackson. Recall too the extraordinary attempted secrecy of Jewel, when at 15 he sneaks off at night alone to work at a long, backbreaking job—clearing Lon Quick's 40 acres of trees and stumps—to earn a beloved horse. To remember such incidents is to realize that the Bundrens are full of secrets. Sometimes, like Addie's affair with the minister Whitfield, these are secrets to be taken to the grave, although the hypocritical minister is afraid that the fear of death and divine judgment will wring a confession from Addie before she dies. Or sometimes, for practical reasons, these are secrets to be pulled out as abruptly as a rabbit out of a hat, the way Jewel suddenly shows up with his horse "like he was riding on a big pinwheel" (*AILD*, 119) or Anse appears with Addie's "duck-shaped" (*AILD*, 241) replacement, springing the journey's final secret along with the book's punch line: "Meet Mrs Bundren."

Or, for a grimmer example just prior to this punch line, the family violently springs its secret plot to commit Darl to the asylum. Dewey Dell has learned from Vardaman that Darl was responsible for burning the Gillespies' barn and has sworn Vardaman to secrecy (*AILD*, 198, 215) until she can inform the Gillespies. As a result, her family arranges for Darl's commitment to the asylum to avoid collective financial responsibility for the Gillespies' loss (*AILD*, 215, 220). Darl, thrown and pinned to the ground, looks up at Cash and says, "I thought you would have told me. . . . I never thought you wouldn't have" (*AILD*, 220). Because of Darl's power to intuit others' thoughts and our own access to his mind, the reader may feel like replying, "I thought you would have known, Darl, and told me. I never thought you wouldn't have." The novel, like the Bundrens, keeps its secrets and to the end retains its power to surprise us.

The fact that the Bundrens have so many private motivations that they keep secret from each other, then, is itself important in understanding Dewey Dell, Jewel, and the others not just as separate characters but as what they are as a secretive family unit, as Bundrens.

More extraordinary is that combined with these habits of stealth is a seemingly preternatural ability at times to pierce through to what the other person is thinking privately. Darl, we just recalled, demonstrates this ability most dramatically—and most disturbingly, to others like Dewey Dell. As Tull observes, "It's like he had got into the inside of you someway" (*AILD*, 111). But others have this capacity as well, as when Darl and Dewey Dell and Darl and Cash speak to each other without words (e.g., *AILD*, 24). Darl's description of the family's sudden fear that something has happened to Jewel, when he briefly disappears before revealing his horse, points more broadly to the Bundrens' habitual complicity in furtiveness. Darl indicates as well how dramatic it is in the Bundren world for the private to become public, as by telepathy or clairvoyance: "It was as though, so long as the deceit ran along quiet and monotonous, all of us let ourselves be deceived, abetting it unawares or maybe through cowardice. . . . But now it was like we had all—and by a kind of telepathic agreement of admitted fear—flung the whole thing back like covers on the bed and we all sitting bolt upright in our nakedness, staring at one another and saying, 'Now is the truth' " (*AILD*, 119). Evidently Darl, too, unconsciously desires or needs not to use his intuitive powers to detect the family plot against him after he burns the barn. Perhaps he lets himself be deceived because it would be too painful for him to believe that his family, even Cash, is capable of turning against him to this extent.

The whole burial journey itself best dramatizes the traumatic eruption of privacy and secrecy into public view. The most secret and private of persons, Addie, is turned into a shocking public spectacle, outraging both public and private life.

All this suggests that what is most important in this novel is not the "secret and selfish" individual psychology alone but the stressful, ambivalent interplay between the private and the public dimensions of human life. This interplay embraces the space and time of "in-between," the transitions, gaps, and overlaps in which the novel operates as the Bundren journey takes place between Addie's dying and burial. It embraces such interplays and overlaps as those between family and society, life and death, religion and economics, and telling and hearing or reading stories. The private lives of the characters exist within their life as a group for whom privacy is a cardinal virtue. Placing its readers at the stress points of a double (individual and collective) existence, the novel allows us to read the power of private and collective lives to shape each other.

If this book is "a outrage," then, how exactly is its outrageousness related to such interplay between private and public existence? What's the point of the novel's outrageousness?

To ask these questions is to look further into the question of what kind of book this is. The beginning of one possible answer is that *As I Lay Dying* is one of Faulkner's family novels. Faulkner was something of a literary specialist in family and social dynamics, his fiction laying open the interactive psychology of families, larger groups, and entire communities.

Faulkner, who was well aware of giving metaphorical names to his characters, uses a surname in this novel that perhaps indicates this focus on the collective or, more exactly, the focus on the individual as part of the family and both as part of the whole social body, the body politic. That is, Faulkner may be playing on more than the resemblance of *burden* and *Bundren* (though in a later novel, *Light in August*, a major character *is* named Joanna Burden), as is suggested by the fact that he used the name *Bunden* (without the *r*) in a short story, "Adolescence," which was an early warm-up for *As I Lay Dying*. This fact helps us to recognize that *Bundren* also plays on *bund*, a somewhat unusual word meaning an organized group, especially for political purposes—a league, a confederation—and related etymologically to *bundle, band, bind,* and *bond.* In another subsequent novel, *Absalom, Absalom!*, Faulkner similarly plays on characters named *Bon* ("good") and *Bond*, that which holds together but also constricts freedom.

Although the word *bund*, of German origin, is somewhat unusual, the connection is not far-fetched. Besides the plentiful evidence we have of Faulkner's wide vocabulary of vernacular and standard English, we know that it would not have been difficult for him to encounter the German cognate *bund*. It appeared in names for everything from banks to armed groups—in newspapers in the United States and Canada, where Faulkner was stationed during World War I, and in newspapers published in Europe during his travels there in 1925. During the war years and the twenties the papers were full of news about dramatic political and economic events involving Germany that formed the basis for Hitler's coming into power following the 1929–30 worldwide economic crash. (The relative familiarity of the word at the time is also suggested by the formation of a friendship league in the United States called the German-American Bund in 1932.) The political resonance of the novel is reinforced by *Vardaman* and *Whitfield*, names of actual political figures in Mississippi, quite important men either actively or symbolically at about the time the story is set.

Whether by conscious design or not, then, the combination of *bund* and *burden* in *Bundren* sums up the novel's interest in family politics that suggest those of society, particularly the relationship between social bonds and burdens. These are bonds of solidarity that help the group to carry its burdens, but they are also burdens in themselves, including everything from certain emotional and intellectual attachments to the religious, economic, and political ties entwined with the personal ones. Secrecy is one such key oppressive family link.

In *As I Lay Dying*, though each family member has his or her own motive for continuing—or in Darl's case, eventually resisting—the burial journey, their dogged persistence as a group is greater than the sum of its individual parts. Their journey develops its own momentum because, as the novel enables us to understand, a group's mentality has its own reality over and above that of the members' separate psychologies. In fact, this is a somewhat misleading way to put the matter, since the group's and the individual's psychologies exist in terms of each other.

To be born into a family like the Bundrens means, among other things, to absorb from birth its habits of secrecy. Each new family member then reinforces the family habit with the others. Secrecy begets more secrecy, in a kind of burdensome bund of mutual concealment. The Bundrens become a clan in being clandestine, held to each other in their shared habit of fiercely holding apart from each other certain cherished individual desires or needs. No wonder there is such burdensome tension among them. The tension of this ambivalent confederation goes far toward making them the Bundrens they are.

Although one would hope that families would develop healthier psychological practices than the Bundren obsession with secrecy, the general point is that every family over the years constructs an entire shared way of life of its own from the mutually dependent actions and reactions that develop between the family members. This way of life is a subculture, with forms of belief and behavior that form the people who live them daily, and it has an internal politics in miniature, with its own ideas of power and justice, might and right.

An almost schematic example is the impact that the conflict between Addie and Anse has on Addie's attitudes toward the children, which in turn affects the attitudes of all the family members toward each other. Addie reacts to Anse's arid conventionality by having a clandestine affair with the minister Whitfield. After this secret liaison produces Jewel, Addie the former schoolteacher provides us with a stern lesson in her sense of justice, in the form of an equally secret home economics that allocates three children to Anse to balance the two she thinks of as her own, Jewel and her firstborn, Cash: "I gave Anse Dewey Dell to negative Jewel. Then I gave him Vardaman to replace the child I had robbed him of [presumably this is Darl, injured psychologically by Addie's rejection of him, though some critics think Cash is meant here and even this doesn't exhaust the possibilities]. And now he has three children that are his and not mine" (*AILD*, 162). Just as Addie's version of economic justice pairs them here, Dewey Dell, Jewel, Darl, and Vardaman each show psychological bonds with the paired brother or sister, as do the two oldest sons, Darl and Cash, separated by about 10 years from the younger three children. (As an illustration of how Addie's scheme works out, note that nobody but Darl really

31

talks to Vardaman, who is severely shaken by his mother's death and the failure of his family to talk to him and comfort him.) And Jewel is fiercely jealous of Addie's other favorite, Cash, as Darl is jealous of and fascinated by Jewel.

The family's action as a group in the burial journey arises from, continues, and modifies many such complex interactions carried out over time, in the group's ongoing history. The Bundrens act as they do largely because of the way they react, and have reacted in the past, to each other. This is also true of their society, the larger group within which the family group exists as part of an ongoing history.

As a tightrope joins two points by maintaining the highest possible tension between them, the solidarity of the secretive Bundrens depends mainly on its being stretched tight across what they in effect believe is a necessary, though troubling, apartness from each other—as if each were set up, in Addie's words, "to negative" the other. Comparable ambivalent strains bind the family to society and bind the society as well. There are no literal tightropes, in the sense of high wires, in this book. But there are equivalent striking images: the tightly stretched rope that Anse grudgingly uses to pull Dr. Peabody's bulk up the hill to the Bundrens', and the one that Jewel on his horse uses to balance his brothers in the wagon against the powerful current as they attempt the river crossing. Literally and figuratively, all are bound by the tensions between them, and yet Peabody comes to help the family, and Cash and Darl, protective of their younger brother, release the rope to save Jewel from the log bearing down on them.

As a whole, as a bund, the Bundrens interact with society by depending on others' help while maintaining a jealously guarded separateness, even to the point of denying the dependency. This denial emerges in Anse's litany, "We would be beholden to no man" (e.g., *AILD*, 18), an ideal of touchy self-sufficiency he rightly attributes also to Addie (e.g., *AILD*, 181). Of course, for the constantly mooching Anse to insist on this is absurd, and the entire trip demonstrates how much the family needs outside help, just as each of them needs the other's assistance. But the ambivalent desire Anse voices is quite real and general in this society. It is the desire not to be beholden, indebted, to others even while one experiences the mutual dependency and interindebtedness that is the life of humans as social beings. This social being is exactly what Dr. Peabody understands as a result of a lifetime helping others and seeing them in their dependency. In a key passage he describes death itself as fundamentally not an individual occurrence but a social episode: "The nihilists say [death] is the end; the fundamentalists, the beginning; when in reality it is no more than a single tenant or family moving out of a tenement or a town" (*AILD*, 39).

The individualistic ideal is underscored when Addie is visibly moved (*AILD*, 120–22) at Jewel's secret passion to earn the wild horse by his labor alone, in lonely agony. She empathizes with Jewel's passion for the free-spirited horse and with Jewel's independence in getting it. She does so even though, as critics agree and Addie seems to sense, the horse is a substitute for Addie, or more exactly what some psychologists call a transitional object, providing Jewel with a means to make a transition from the exclusiveness of his and Addie's intense mutual attachment. But it should be noted that although Jewel's individual effort is indeed heroic, neither he nor Addie acknowledges his beholdenness to his brothers and sister, who by doing Jewel's daily chores have given him considerable help to keep his secret effort going. And despite his proud claim that he will kill the horse rather than have to depend on Anse to feed it (*AILD*, 121), our first view of Jewel and the horse together shows him sneaking the horse extra food from the common family supply: "Clinging to the hay-rack [Jewel] lowers his head and peers out. . . . The path is empty. . . . He reaches up and drags down hay in hurried armsful and crams it into the rack. 'Eat,' he says. 'Get the goddam stuff out of sight while you got a chance' " (*AILD*, 12).

Pointing to such contradictory hyperindividualism by no means denies that some, like Addie, have relatively more independent characters than others; nor does it deny, for instance, that the Tulls represent farming families who have achieved habits of successful relative self-reliance. The point is that, from a lazy Anse to an energetic Jewel or Addie, by words or other behavior there is an excessive claim to extreme self-sufficiency. To a significant extent, the claim is a social fiction voicing a socially powerful desire. During the journey Jewel even comically projects this desire onto his beloved horse when Samson offers to feed him. "He aint never been beholden to no man," Jewel says, to which Samson answers, "Then it's high time he commenced" (*AILD*, 102).

Again, others may object in this way to the false Bundren pride and may smile at the contradiction between Anse's habitual claim and the well-known fact that Anse defines the word *beholden*. But when Anse attaches such overt claims to his displays of ineptitude and helplessness, oddly enough, he speaks the language of their desire. He effectively draws upon the power of what all after their fashion want to believe: that in their own mutual dependency and their vulnerability to flood, drought, and economic oppression, they still remain proudly autonomous and powerful. In presenting them a sort of fun-house mirror image of this desired conviction, Anse is in effect telling them what they want to hear, and so he has an apparently mysterious power over them: "Be durn if there aint something about a durn fellow like Anse that seems to make a man have to help him, even when he knows he'll be wanting to kick himself next minute. . . . I be durn if Anse dont conjure a man, some way" (*AILD*, 179).

Whether conjuring help or outraging decorum, the Bundrens embody their society's habits, which the family can conjure or outrage not because their own practices are essentially different but because they are a ten-power magnification of social practice, detailing its cross-grains. In this way Anse, as well as the Bundren family as a whole, is the typically Faulknerian apparent misfit or anomaly in society who actually is a blowup of some of its key features, a living commentary on the conflicts intrinsic to its clannish solidarity. (Other examples are Joe Christmas in *Light in August*, Thomas Sutpen in *Absalom, Absalom!*, and Flem Snopes in *The Hamlet*.)

The novel is built on the simple device of a journey demanding cooperative action that simultaneously displays the high-tension family and social solidarity at work and threatens to snap it. Faulkner amplifies this effect by making this a journey of death, death being the event that apparently epitomizes the individuality of existence—in the end, it's often said, we die alone. What's more, Faulkner makes this the death of an impressively independent-minded person. And yet, as Peabody indicates, the novel emphasizes how much death itself is a phase of social existence. As for aloneness, or loneliness, the text underscores how much this is characteristic of not only death but also life and, further, how much it is a product of a social cult of hyperindividualism and secrecy.

The interplay between the Bundrens' loyalties and selfishness, jealousies and admirations, abilities and disabilities, energy and passivity, secrets and nakedness, guilts, shames, and loves results in a journey neither Anse nor any of them could have accomplished as an individual. But partly because the journey's stubborn momentum develops within the family's relationships, lodging not so much within each character as within a rickety semblance of cooperation, that momentum seems to take on a life of its own. It veers beyond control into outrageous sequences or combinations of craziness and heroism—sometimes as we read we don't know whether to laugh, cry, applaud, or wrinkle our noses, or try to do all at once: "a outrage."

At times this family novel reads like an epic journey, in keeping with the source of the title, the "Book of the Dead" in Homer's epic of Odysseus' journey to return to his family and society. "As I lay dying" are the words spoken in Hades by Agamemnon, Odysseus' former military commander, recounting his own homecoming murder by his wife, whom Agamemnon had earlier himself betrayed by sacrificing their daughter's life for what he thought was the good of society. Faulkner typically rearranges such sources and plays variations on the original themes. In this novel he switches the roles of husband and wife by making Addie the one who is dying, but he makes her the center of a web of mutual betrayals and revenges running throughout the family and extending beyond. And he sends the whole conflicting family on a journey to return Addie to her original family, her "blood," in the town graveyard.

At times the novel reads like a tragedy—say, a revision of Sophocles' *Antigone*, the drama of a sister's persistent attempt to have her brother buried, against the opposition of her royal uncle, Creon. The king champions what he believes are the needs of society as a whole over the traditional family responsibility to bury the dead—and finally has Antigone buried alive instead.

Famous Greeks aside, at times (or at the same time) the book reads like a comic strip version of American, old Southwestern, frontier humor: broadly cartoonish, physical, and heavily threaded with gallows humor. The novel's grotesquery specifically recalls the tales of the impudent, earthy Sut Lovingood, a favorite of Faulkner, who praised this unconventional trickster for traits the very opposite of Anse's blaming and whining.

*As I Lay Dying* omits such a trickster figure as Sut, but the gallows humor of the novel recalls Sut's spirit of irreverence, aroused by solemn occasions. This mood is akin to the embarrassing temptation to smile or laugh that can afflict some people at funeral services, when the grievousness of death momentarily can appear rather comical because the exaggerated ceremonies or atmosphere of reverence turn what ought to be moving into something faintly ridiculous. This is not to say that the Bundrens, even Anse, don't feel loss or grief at Addie's death. But Anse's attempt to stage-manage the entire sequence of Addie's funeral and burial journey repeatedly invites the laughter-at-the-funeral reaction to his grieving demeanor, a "monstrous burlesque of all bereavement" (*AILD*, 69), and to his fussy propriety on the journey, as in his objecting to Cash's bringing his tools, Dewey Dell her package, and Jewel his horse. Darl's unsettling laughter at Anse and at the entire charade is our cue. Beyond Anse, the whole burial journey can make the reader feel the flickering of nervous laughter at the clashing of its would-be unbroken solemnity, its actual mixed motives and conflicts, and the increasing awfulness of the corpse's disintegration.

For a writer to attempt such outrageous mixtures of epic storytelling, tragedy, and grotesque humor is extremely risky. To do it successfully means that he or she must suggest that the outrageous mixtures of reverence and risibility, sentiment and sass, are not haphazard but somehow meaningful and even necessary. For in reading, while we may seldom want to classify formally the kind of literature we are holding in our hands, we often do want to get the sense that it all adds up to an intellectual and emotional perspective, that it adopts an attitude, however complex. For instance, we might feel that one novel is a disillusioned book about war. Or another a lightly funny treatment of serious problems of love. Or another a romantic but streetwise detective thriller. And so on.

With a discomforting novel like *As I Lay Dying*, however, we may be hard pressed to decide what exactly is its overall attitude, its tone, and we may wonder at its shocking "contents" somewhat in the spirit of "Great God, what they got in that wagon?" Faulkner's remark about the tightrope between the bizarre and the terrible has prompted us to consider this decision first in general terms of the inherent potential humor in tragedy and tragedy in humor, so the line between them can dissolve, as if we emitted an embarrassing giggle at a funeral.

Further, we have begun to relate this volatility of tone specifically to the novel's themes and issues. We still have ample reason to ask, however, what exactly there is in the bizarreness and terribleness of this specific novel, *As I Lay Dying*, that brings comedy and tragedy close together and combines realist and nonrealist narrative. The real point here is not to classify the whole novel in some traditional genre, perhaps a hybrid like tragicomedy, since to do so now might make us content with mere classification—click, mentally file away and click, soon forget: tragicomic family novel. The point is to ask how this text's hybrid mixtures—or, if you prefer the irreverent spirit of a Sut Lovingood, its mongrel combinations—make sense and "work" for many readers.

For a writer to produce a novel that raises this and related questions meaningfully without producing mere chaos requires considerable skill in the techniques of fiction. No wonder that Faulkner spoke of this text in terms of its technical achievements, as a tour de force, a display of a performer's skills. The family's persistence and the resulting outrageousness of the story's incidents, though striking and significant, are not by themselves the reasons that *As I Lay Dying* is meaningfully outrageous. A major contribution is also made by the book's other outrageousness, starting with the way that the story is told and the meanings of this telling.

In the particular way that this novel shows off on its tightrope, it shows us not just lives but a way of life—and death. The tightrope image emphasizes that, both literally and figuratively, this is a novel of a hazardous journey, a dangerous transition between places and between states of being. The novel deals with, and itself exemplifies, what is in-between and mixed. To be in-between is to be neither securely here nor there but in transition between them. It is also to be in something like Addie's condition, which is neither (conventionally understood) life nor death but something in-between, neither safely this nor that, but something that falls disturbingly into the cracks of conventional words and ideas. It is to be in between "twenties/Southern individualism" and "thirties/ Southern collectivism." To be in-between in these ways and others is to be potentially outrageous.


## READING THE WAY THE STORY IS TOLD


Suppose we were asked to tell about *As I Lay Dying* and we started like this: As the novel opens in a small Mississippi farm one summer during the twenties, Addie Bundren lies on her bed dying. Awaiting her death or resisting the thought of it are her husband, Anse, and their children: Vardaman, about 7 or 8 years old, Dewey Dell, 17, Jewel, about 18, and Darl and Cash, in their late twenties. Anse has promised Addie that she will be buried in Jefferson, a town usually about two days travel by wagon (Tull says, page 25, it's a hard day's ride; on page 79, it's said to be two to three days). Addie apparently has one or more concealed motives for getting Anse to make this promise. Years before, she became furious at Anse for deceiving her with declarations of love into having a second child, Darl. And apparently she has other reasons as well. At any rate, knowing that lazy Anse tries to avoid any effort and particularly hates to travel, as a means of revenge she asks him to make a promise she knows will cause him trouble. As it turns out, a hard rain and consequent flooding of the river compounds the trouble enormously, so nine days pass after Addie's death before they get to Jefferson. Actually, however, Anse is using his promise in order to go to Jefferson for his own purposes, most obviously to get false teeth and a new wife to replace Addie. Similarly, Dewey Dell, who has secretly become pregnant by a young man named Lafe, also wants to go to Jefferson for her own reason: to buy something to induce an abortion.

What can we say of this partial summary so far? Accurate enough in certain details, it has the virtue, arguably, of focusing on the conflict between Addie and Anse and highlighting Anse's incongruous ability to turn situations to his advantage. But it has problems as well. For one thing, as the preceding discussion has suggested, this standard sort of summary concentrates too much on each family member's separate motives, at the expense of indicating the family subculture at work as part of the surrounding culture. For another thing, notice that after the note in parentheses the summary implies that the novel makes all these motives pretty clear from the first, when in fact we learn them piecemeal or in one of the novel's surprise revelations. In other words, this account ignores the way—the quietly bizarre way—the novel opens. This second objection is related to the first, and both tell us that what is needed is a more carefully detailed reading of the opening sections in the context of the whole book.

Actually, as the narrative begins with a section labelled "Darl," someone, presumably Darl, rather meticulously narrates the walk that he and someone named Jewel take from the field to the house, in the course of which Jewel unhesitatingly walks through the opposing windows of the cotton house instead of following the path around it. Darl "sees" Jewel do this even though Darl is 15 feet ahead of him on the path. Only at the end of this brief account is there any mention of Addie Bundren and, indirectly, of her impending death, and it comes in Darl's assessment of the coffin someone named Cash is building: "Addie Bundren could not want a better . . . box to lie in. It will give her confidence and comfort" (*AILD*, 4). Darl, strangely, does not call her his mother, only "Addie Bundren." Only later does their relationship become clear. Further, her (oddly implied) death is given little more explicit attention than any number of other things Darl observes with great precision about these unusually named people, including the sound of Cash's adze as it cuts the planks, represented by the word "Chuck" and its unusual typographical spacing on the page.

Next we have a section labeled "Cora," in which Cora (1) on religious grounds justifies herself against a "rich" woman in town who wouldn't buy the cake Cora baked, and (2) on economic grounds mentally rehearses a justification of her actions to her husband. In the course of this microeconomic accounting of eggs, hens, and flour by Cora, she abruptly begins to describe someone she calls "her" lying in bed covered with a quilt on the hot day. We can infer that this is Addie, for whom the coffin is being built. Only much later will we be able to see the connection between Cora's thoughts and her observation of Addie here: Cora is implicitly contrasting her own self-justification with what she believes is Addie's lack of justification before God (*AILD*, 152–54).

Then Darl narrates another section—first, detailing a sensuous, sensual childhood memory awakened by a bucket of water, and second, dramatically describing Jewel and his horse, whom Darl sees as bound together by Jewel's violent, quasi-sexual attachment. Despite Darl's detailed description, neither Jewel nor the horse is visible from where Darl is. Again, Darl "sees" what he cannot physically see, although the description is so vivid that a first reading may overlook this fact, and a commonsense explanation is readily available: this is a description of what Jewel usually does.

The next section is narrated by Jewel (the only one he will narrate, we eventually learn), who with at times almost incoherent fury tells of his jealous outrage that Cash is building "that goddam box" (*AILD*, 13) where "she" (Addie, we infer) can see him; that visitors are sitting like buzzards surrounding Addie; and ultimately that he and Addie cannot be, as he fantasizes, alone together after Jewel violently drives everyone else away.

By the 1920s, incidentally, the once-common Southern rural practice of building coffins for one's own family had become uncommon, but Cash's activity is likely to strike the modern reader as, at least, downright eccentric as first Darl and then Jewel describe it. In relation to the whole novel, we can see that Faulkner begins to accomplish a number of aims here. For example, on the one hand, by so strongly emphasizing from the first that the Bundrens build their own coffin, Faulkner begins to make their poverty clear. An act of piety, building a coffin, is also an act of economics, an association Faulkner begins quietly to build with Cora's hodgepodge of economics and religiosity. On the other hand, because of the way Faulkner presents the coffin building through Darl's and Jewel's reactions, he nevertheless begins to suggest that the Bundren desire for either the appearance or the reality of such family self-sufficiency extends to the point of weirdness and obsession.

Reviewing the way the novel really begins, we notice that it seems to sidle up to the idea of Addie's death by way of others' various related or unrelated odd actions and preoccupations. In these preoccupations the idea of her death is either set off-center or overwhelmed—for instance, by Jewel's jealous mental violence against those he sees in competition for Addie, by Darl's observation of Cash carefully building her coffin before her eyes, or by Cora's defensive self-justification. We notice, to put it another way, the novel's extraordinary reliance on delaying important information and instead presenting vivid fragments. Only an alert, imaginative reading can gradually put these reports together into a larger understanding, but even so, much that we need to know is revealed only later, as in a mystery story.

For instance, we learn only subsequently, and gradually, about Anse's desire to get teeth in Jefferson, first indicated obscurely in Darl's clairvoyant report of Anse's cryptic comment on Addie's death, "Now I can get them teeth" (*AILD*, 48). And of course, though a hint is dropped by Kate Tull, Anse's motive of obtaining a new wife is revealed openly only at the end of the novel. Another, subtler example involves Jewel's behavior in walking straight through the building's windows, which introduces us to his characteristic undeviating determination, impatience, and relative unconcern for conventionality. These traits, along with his passionate, violent attachments—to his mother and to an active natural being, his horse—ally him closely with his mother's personality, though this will not become clear until Addie's section many pages later. Jewel, we learn later, is one of Addie's two favorites; Cash is the other child whom Addie claims as her own and whom Jewel resents for that reason.

Darl, it is gradually revealed, is a rejected son and so feels that he really has no mother; his calling her "Addie Bundren" is, as we look back, our first tip-off. Nevertheless, Darl's associations with and sensitivity to water, which we come to realize tie in with his fascination with things dissolving, subsequently link him to his mother's sensuous and sensual visions of life as blood flowing through the land. So do the poetic visions created by Darl's clairvoyance. Later Darl will describe his mother's death even though he is miles away with Jewel, and details of his description will be confirmed by Peabody, physically present at her death. Cash too is very much his mother's son in expressing his feelings through physical action rather than through words—as an adult stoically building a coffin for the mother he loves and, in Jewel's jealous memory, as a child bringing her manure in a bread pan because she mentioned that she wished she had fertilizer for flowers.

This discussion makes clear that, contrary to what that initial summary implied, the novel delays revelation of Addie's individual motivations and much of her important relationship to her children and husband, until we encounter her sole narrated section two-thirds of the way through the novel. Even so, we might wonder if "revelation" is the right word for the indirect, impressionistic presentation of her rationale, which, on first reading at least, raises almost as many questions as it clarifies. (For instance, some critics have denied that Addie obtains Anse's promise as revenge.) Of course, some delaying of information is standard practice in narrative. But this novel extraordinarily suspends its readers in a succession of partial, often abrupt glimpses that only gradually begin to crystallize into something like a whole.

There are a number of persuasive answers to the question of why it makes sense for the novel to be written this way. There is, for example, the general point about creating suspense and dramatic effect, but this applies too broadly to fiction to pinpoint why such storytelling techniques are fitting here. A more interesting because more specific answer is that this method puts readers in a position similar to that of the Bundrens, being bound together by secretiveness. We too are drawn to this family by the sense of important things withheld from us, like secrets, even while we can look into their minds and occasionally, like clairvoyants, gain sudden revelations that pierce the secrecy, rather like what the Bundrens do with one another. Thus, for readers with a sufficient tolerance for delayed information, reading this novel means "participating in" the Bundren clandestine world by acting it out; on the whole, however, we participate with more pleasure than they, as we struggle with and find satisfaction in the narrative's well-kept (and well-sprung) secrets.

We have been noticing how much this novel not only delays information about individual motives but, at the same time, apparently sets off-center its ostensible subject, announced in the title—the death of "I," of Addie—by refracting it through everyone else's preoccupations. However, there is another way of thinking about this method of storytelling than solely in terms of delay and indirection. It is possible that at the same time the novel delays some matters, it also redirects us, its readers, to a different conception of death, and with it a different conception of the "I," the individual life, as well. In other words, after the title of the novel creates the expectation that it will deal with the dying "I," maybe the novel is doing just that, by focusing on matters leading us to a revised idea of its subject, which our conventional expectations about death can make us misunderstand as strangely irrelevant.

In fact, on first, conventional encounter, even the book's title is impossible. How can the speaker refer to the speaker's own death in the past tense? In standard English, the "lay" of the title indicates the past tense, although colloquial usage, like the characters in this novel, often violates this rule in phrases like "lay down." Or perhaps, we may think when we first read the title, this is a tale of the supernatural. But upon reading the novel we discover that this is not, for example, the preternatural horror fiction of an Edgar Allan Poe—although Faulkner's novel is macabre enough in its own way. Nor is it a lengthy flashback compressed into the pinpoint instant of death.

The title begins to intimate what the whole book will tell us, that we cannot apply to it the most conventional understanding of what "I" and "dying" are. Amplifying our initial analysis of the Bundrens as a microcosm of their society, we as readers might work toward this conclusion along the following lines. With a nudge from the paradoxical title and Dr. Peabody's thoughts on death, we may begin to speculate that dying in this novel is not to be understood as a single moment limited to a single person but as a protracted process taking place within a group. Addie's death, then, includes her final illness and burial journey and occurs through and within others. From the first page of the book, in other words, we *are* reading of Addie's death when we begin to read of how her present condition impinges or fails to impinge on others' thoughts, feelings, and actions.

Dr. Peabody's opinion, helping us to form this hypothesis, is impressive if for no other reason initially than that we encounter it early, as the first serious philosophical statement in the novel: "I can remember how when I was young I believed death to be a phenomenon of the body; now I know it to be merely a function of the mind—and that of the minds of the ones who suffer the bereavement" (*AILD*, 39). Applied specifically to Addie, this idea draws our attention to the way that she, though dead, continues to live in the minds of her family, even continues to speak to them, and yet also gradually diminishes in their minds, in a protracted process of dying. But Peabody is talking about everyone, not just Addie, and as we read further the other characters' inescapable connections and entanglements with each other become clearer. How much they are functions of each others' minds is spotlighted by this sharing in the death process and by the journey's demand for cooperation. This observation gives new meaning to Peabody's implication that his statement applies not only to death but to death and life as a continuity. For he began by saying of Addie's long final illness, "She cannot even make that change, if change it be," and he later adds, as previously noted, "The nihilists say it is the end, the fundamentalists, the beginning; when in reality it is no more than a single tenant or family moving out of a tenement or a town" (*AILD*, 39).

These thoughts go far toward confirming and generalizing the hypothesis developed here: Not only one's death but one's life happens in and through others, as an episode within the "tenement or town" of the group's life as a whole. This provides another explanation for the fact that in the center of the novel Cora, Addie, and Whitfield suddenly speak outside the chronological sequence, as if abruptly disclosing secrets after Addie's physical demise. This arresting trio of speeches, like other features of the novel, emphasizes that in the collective life and death, nothing happens only once. Actions and identities continue to echo in other actions and identities, emerging unexpectedly with continuing power after common sense or forgetfulness has consigned them to "past history."

Nevertheless, it is strikingly significant that although the family members are deeply involved in the group's thoughts and lives, this involvement is combined with their equally powerful mutual alienation. They need each other and can momentarily reach extraordinary intimacy, but they are also isolated, strangers to each other. Similarly notable is their ambivalence toward their loneliness, as in Dewey Dell's eloquent formulation of her pregnancy as a terrifying "process of coming unalone" within herself (*AILD*, 56). Their doubts about their identities are also arresting. Darl's doubt is the most evident: "I dont know what I am. I dont know if I am or not" (*AILD*, 72). But there is something similar, for instance, in Dewey Dell's nightmare: "*I couldn't think of my name I couldn't even think I am a girl I couldn't even think I*" (*AILD*, 107).

This doubt is there too, indirectly, in Vardaman's need to try to reassure himself of the boundary between his "I" and that of Jewel's horse as it seems to dissolve in the darkness: "an *is* different from my *is*" (*AILD*, 52).

From this perspective, then, life, death, and the "I" itself would seem actually to exist *inter*subjectively, as a set of relationships between physically separate subjects, or individuals. A crucial point is that nothing in this interactive process of group life per se denies individuality, in the sense that each "I" is distinctive. Rather, the process defines a certain understanding of what individuality is. Each person's specific individuality exists dynamically, in the distinctive way each lives out the cluster of relationships. Vardaman, in his childish—and mind-boggling—way, tries to get at this distinction between his and Jewel's relationships with their mother: "Jewel's mother is a horse. My mother is a fish" (*AILD*, 182). We must note, however, that *individual* would be an inappropriate word if we meant it in its literal root sense of "not dividable," because this novel, like much modern thought, describes an "I" significantly divided within itself. But because individualism is a key issue in the novel, we may continue to use familiar terms like *individual* to refer to the distinctiveness each "I" nevertheless has.

Yet, despite the actuality of the individual identity within the group's corporate life, the feeling of threatened individuality is still strong in this novel's world. We can conclude that the pervasive loneliness, self-doubt, and ambivalent hunger for satisfying connection is related to the fact that this society, as noted before, places its own troublesome *interpretation* on individual distinctiveness. In stressing an ideal of private self-sufficiency, it teaches an exaggerated standard of "rugged individualism," exaggerated because it is supposed to apply sweepingly to your emotional as well as your practical life. From the standpoint of this extreme ideal, stressful situations like an unwelcome pregnancy, the death of a mother, or a dangerous journey, which make your psychological and practical dependency all too obvious, may seem to expose the inadequacy of your individuality. You experience a painful loneliness, long to lose it, yet dread to do so; you "would be beholden" to nobody else.

A family largely formed by this ambivalence and contradiction, the Bundrens act out a self-sufficiency that is its own self-parody.

They act out the unwitting parody in Anse's denial of debt to others, as when he needs a mule team to replace the one lost in the river crossing. Before the crossing, if Tull had agreed, Anse was quite ready to borrow (and risk drowning) Tull's mule to help cross the river. And after the crossing, Anse's rhetorical mixture of poor mouth and pride has made his later host, Armstid, ready to lend him his team. But in a display of futile "self-sufficiency" and a mockery of family cooperation, Anse insists on trading for mules with a sharp-trading Snopes by stealing the money Cash saved to buy a phonograph, in effect robbing Jewel of his horse, and burdening his family with a mortgage on their farm equipment.

Comparably, the young, uninformed Dewey Dell, unable to ask for psychological or practical support from family, friends, or even Dr. Peabody, attempts an independent search for help that leaves her dependent and vulnerable to sexual exploitation by townsman Skeet MacGowan. Vardaman, a child offered far too little comfort or help in understanding his mother's death and as a result deeply disturbed, relies upon his own self-sufficient—and thus unintentionally absurd—comforting explanation for her disappearance, his fish story. That it cannot stand alone is clear from his determined efforts to get some confirmation of his story from Vernon Tull.

Jewel's claim to utter independence is contradicted, as noted before, but Jewel impresses readers as such a strong personality that he deserves more attention here. His desire for self-sufficiency takes the form of impatience for immediate independent action. This impatient desire is full of tortured feelings of resentment and confusion at both being a Bundren and yet, because of Darl's insinuations about Jewel's father if nothing else, suspecting dimly that he is not entirely one. (Dewey Dell's early view that he is "not kin to us in caring" is also relevant; *AILD*, 23.) So Jewel wants to act in defiant independence from his family and yet in this very independence win his spurs as more Bundren than the Bundrens. His moment of most triumphant self-sufficient action is his single-handed rescue of Addie's coffin from the barn Darl set on fire. It is also the most ironic because, as Cash observes, surely by this time Addie's memory would have been best served by wise inaction, allowing her grotesque remains to be destroyed cleanly. Jewel's act of heroic individualism is tellingly perverse in showing how much he has made a fetish of his emotional dependency on his mother.

On this tightrope of a journey, Cash is in many ways the most balanced Bundren, with his quiet, justified pride in his individual craftsmanship in carpentry, which he uses to contribute to the common effort. But by the novel's end, Cash, so concerned that the coffin won't balance, will have not only broken his leg in his second major accident in a year but has ensured that it is crippled. Although after he breaks his leg in the river crossing he becomes an additional burden rather than a help, instead of stopping at Armstid's house or in Mottson for healing and proper medical help, he insists on enduring for several days the pain of the jolting wagon and so makes himself permanently handicapped. This is a bizarre display of stoic self-sufficiency both as an individual and a member of a putatively self-sufficient family. Riding directly on top of the coffin's stench, Cash forms one bookend image of futilely heroic self-sufficiency and underlying dependency to match the other image—that of Jewel with the coffin riding on his back as he carries this burden from the burning barn.

As for Darl, he tries throughout the novel to maintain the extreme mental detachment that is his form of self-sufficiency. The capping image of the potential self-parody in this and all the Bundrens' comparable efforts is his final destination, the insane asylum. The inmates of this social institution combine terrible isolation with total dependency as wards of the state. Here the tendencies of the Bundren family as social institution are reduced to absurdity.

The novel accentuates the admirable streak of gritty independence in these country people (think, for instance, of the child Vardaman trudging miles through the night storm to get Tull to confirm Vardaman's bizarre fish story). Because of the overall form this independence takes, however, the Bundrens' outright heroism becomes indistinguishable from outright mania and their independent streak from a streak of collective insanity, even though only one Bundren is officially committed.

In rereading the opening chapters as a preview, we have noticed another important cultural mentality related to this sort of individualism. This mentality takes the form of what at first looks like a pure contrast between Jewel's temperament and outlook and Cora Tull's, and between Bundren and non-Bundren. Cora's egg-by-hen calculation that her planned cake sale would allow her to "earn enough at one time to increase the net value of the flock the equivalent of two head" (*AILD*, 5) mingles with her religiously expressed resentments against the town woman who "same as gave . . . her word" to buy them but didn't. This calculating resentment doesn't stop at the town woman. When her daughter Kate says, "Those rich town ladies can change their minds. Poor folks cant," Cora thinks, "Riches is nothing in the face of the Lord, for He can see into the heart. . . . If it is His will that some folks has different ideas of honesty from other folks, it is not my place to question His decree" (*AILD*, 6). Cora, in her sharpness of tone, does the very thing she denies doing, questioning what she sees as God's will, at least the part she doesn't like—God's allowing dishonesty to exist. She does so even while she as a poor woman identifies with the part of the divine will she does like—God's power to punish the rich—and mentally threatens the town woman with this power.

This passage gives us, among other things, a foretaste of Cora's hypocritical conventionality. As when Cora goes about confidently singing of "bounding toward my God and my reward" in heaven (*AILD*, 82–83), the impression given is that for her, religion fundamentally means winning the jackpot after death. It means living in anticipation of collecting the profits of a lifetime of prudent long-term spiritual investments—much like the better grade of chickens she urged on Vernon, which "pays in the long run" (*AILD*, 5)—and pleasurably turning the tables on those, primarily the rich townsfolk, who have enjoyed prosperity in earthly life. As her husband Vernon cautiously observes, "I reckon it does take a powerful trust in the Lord to guard a fellow, though sometimes I think that Cora's a mite over-cautious, like she was trying to crowd the other folks away and get in closer than anybody else" (*AILD*, 63).

Equally, Cora's first narrated section subtly points toward Vernon's understanding of her desire for Godlike power. As he ruefully says, "I reckon if there's ere a man or woman anywhere that He could turn it all over to and go away with His mind at rest, it would be Cora. And I reckon she would make a few changes no matter how He was running it. And I reckon they would be for man's good. Leastways, we would have to like them. Leastways, we might as well go on and make like we did" (*AILD*, 66). Droll humor like this shouldn't keep us from noticing the serious point being made. Here we see that Vernon Tull too questions at the same time

48

as he yields to divine might even Cora's power as a would-be substitute God, and this along with other evidence suggests that though kind, put-upon Tull is no hypocrite, his wife's outlook on power is not wholly foreign to his own.

Near the opening of the novel Jewel expresses a resentful, envious desire like Cora's, though his furious obscurity can make it easy to miss what he is saying: "*If it had just been me* when Cash fell off of that church *and if it had just been me* when pa laid sick with that load of wood fell on him, it would not be happening with every bastard in the country coming in to stare at her *because if there is a God what the hell is He for.* It would just be me and her on a high hill and me rolling the rocks down the hill at their faces, picking them up and throwing them down the hill faces and teeth and all by God . . ." (*AILD*, 13–14; italics added). By God, indeed. Put in plain language, what Jewel is thinking but not daring to spell out even to himself is that if he had been God when Cash and Anse had their accidents, he would have killed them as a substitute for Addie's death, and then Addie would not lie dying while she is watched by people like Cora. Jewel's hatred of Cora and her kind aside, an important similarity with Cora emerges here, all the more important because Jewel and Cora are so different as individuals. The key similarity in their thinking is thus revealed not as an individually unique pattern but as a culturally shared habit.

As Vernon Tull senses that Cora does, Jewel plays God. With her mix of earthly and heavenly economics, Cora swaps around in her mind eggs and flour and God's power over condescending town women. Comparably, Jewel's economics mentally trades the death of Cash and Anse for Addie's. Like Cora, Jewel engages in desired symbolic exchanges and substitutions, trades and trade-offs, in order psychologically to control and dominate threatening events by creating in himself a feeling of power, the power of a god.

Addie's section subsequently will show that Jewel himself is the product of Addie's union with a minister. To Addie this union connects her with the life power that is God, and she calls Jewel her savior. Thus when Jewel's birth sets off the secret trading of children in Addie's mind, the association of religious and economic thinking recurs. Addie's secret arrangement to keep Cash and Jewel to herself eerily echoes what her opposite in personality, Cora, does in her first narrated section. Addie too justifies herself mentally with her husband, allotting children to herself but making up the difference by allotting the remaining children to him. That she does so even though she is contemptuous of Anse may suggest something of the power of husbands and fathers in the mentality of a communal life that, as the novel repeats several times, is hard on women.

Cora's and Jewel's opening sections, then, eccentrically introduce a central cultural theme, the fusion of economics and religion with a desire for power, and the discontentments of class and gender that fuse them in this society.

Later, in chapter 7, we take up this idea again directly. Already, however, we can see that this novel shows us in microcosm a society that is its own burden by showing us a family that is its own burden. This self-burdening operates in the stressful, ambivalent interplay between the private and the public noted earlier. In this novel, characters live their lives largely inside their heads, but a family and a whole society are in there with them.

The problem with the standard summary given earlier is that it treats this novel as a conventional story. But the novel's subtle and dramatic departures from conventional storytelling invite us to a number of possible reading experiences that are far from conventional. The first summary, apparently straightforward and factual, neglected what can be learned from the actual process of the novel's unfolding, sentence by sentence and page by page, in equal portions of vivid directness and quiet indirection.

The first summary's conventionality failed to capture the novel's highlighting and questioning of conventions—that is, customs and usages, or the general agreements, usually assumed and unspoken, on the usages and practices of social life. Faulkner, in fact, commented on this feature of his novel. When someone in a classroom discussion tentatively proposed Anse as the novel's villain, Faulkner replied, "If there is a villain in that story it's the convention in which people have to live" (Gwynn and Blotner, 112). Conventions are preestablished links between people, pivots for the interplay between public and private. As such, they are stress points in this novel of bonds and burdens. Anse, by dragging his dead wife across the countryside in the name of the most traditional piety for the dead, drags the conventionality of life we take for granted out into the Mississippi July glare of day.

# 5

# "I would be I":
# Fragments of Collective Action

As convention-spouting Anse is the prime representative of a villainous conventionality, Addie is a representative figure of desire or need frustrated by convention. As everyone has some Anse in them, so everyone has some Addie. We shouldn't be misled by real individual differences between Addie and her family into failing to see how representative she is. Again, outrage gives us a way in.

The characteristic Faulknerian emotion of outrage is, at a minimum, the trace of intense feeling remaining in all the characters, even Anse. Outrage is the sense that one's values and self-esteem have been insulted, flouted. It is, in other words, the response of the "I" to a threat against it. In Faulkner's writing, outrage is often passion's last stand even if a passionate vitality has been choked out of the characters' lives in every other form. Because Addie feels that her yearning for life has been so often balked and because it is nevertheless still intractable, she expresses it bitterly, as in her memorable surreal image of the wild blood of all living things as "terrible blood, the red bitter flood boiling through the land" (*AILD*, 161).

Throughout Addie's chapter we can feel her outrage at the violation of her "I" by the conventionality represented in language, as well as her determination to resist this invasion. "I would be I," she vows, contrasting herself to Anse. "I would let him be the shape and echo of his word" (*AILD*, 160). Addie determines to be beyond words, which she disdains because they frustrate the "I" by falsify-

51

ing the ineffable distinctiveness and concreteness of individual experience: "Words dont ever fit even what they are trying to say at. . . . [The word] fear was invented by someone that had never had the fear; pride, who never had the pride" (*AILD*, 157). How, Addie is asking, can such general, preset conventions embody the specific, freshly felt experience of *my* fear, *my* pride, *my* love, or *your* loss, *your* hope? They cannot, she feels, and as a result, words can only accomplish at best a superficial contact between people. Compared to the authentic individual experience, words in themselves, whether or not the speaker is sincere, are deceptions and betrayals of speaker as well as hearer. This is why Anse too, Addie feels, is as much betrayed as betrayer, though she still desires to be revenged on him (*AILD*, 159) and so strike back at the inauthenticity of conventions.

For Addie, "love" in particular is Anse's word, the word he used, she believes, to "trick" her into having her second child, Darl. To Addie, Anse's use of the word "love" is an empty convention that simply goes with marriage and is a mere substitute for having the really unnameable passion; as she puts it, the word is a "shape to fill a lack" (*AILD*, 158). In the context of the whole novel, her phrase "his word" also means the promise Anse gives her. Or rather, as she sees it, this is the word she extracts from him, manipulating Anse by manipulating another key social convention, promising, since she views him as merely an artifact of such conventions.

Addie's words are cryptic, as befits her intense privacy. As Anse says, "she was ever a private woman" (*AILD*, 17). This secretive privacy is part of her desire to live beyond the reach of such conventions as words, but still to use them to affect others, like Anse. It helps us to follow her slippery turns of thought if we notice how, by three parallel phrasings, the text suggests that to her, "wild blood" is the same as, or embodied in, physical, nonverbal actions. First, "I would think how words go straight up in a thin line, quick and harmless, and how terribly doing goes along the earth." Second, "the terrible blood, the red bitter flood boiling through the land." Third, "My children were of me alone, and of the wild blood boiling along the earth" (*AILD*, 160–62).

The blood is natural life itself: it flows in others (*AILD*, 155), Addie says, and she associates it with "the earth," "the land," and the haunting cries of the wild geese (*AILD*, 156) announcing renewed life in the spring. Ultimately, she believes, this wild active blood is God's "voiceless speech," in which "the words are the deeds" (*AILD*, 161, 160). To participate in it means to commune directly with God, whose actions are a life-giving communication transcending conventions like ordinary words. (Addie is harkening back to Genesis 1:3, where God says, "Let there be light," and light is instantly created; in this sense God's words are deeds, actions creating life.) This is the life force Addie wishes to share intensely: in general, with others through her actions; in particular, by physical union with God's designated agent, the minister Whitfield.

At a deeper level, then, Addie is assuming that human words are not deeds because human language lacks the divine power directly to contact, create, and sustain life. But for humans, she feels, actions uniting people physically—especially when they are convention-flouting actions—do allow direct, full participation in this divine lifeblood of the world. Thus she insists that what she does with the minister is a sin—that is, it breaks the conventions, the laws, of their religion—but that like the clothing she and he remove, the sin *is* no more than a convention, one that need not limit those who wish to live authentically, like gods. She implies, in fact, that God's actions in the world break the conventions too, therefore that God sins, when she links "God's love and His beauty and His sin" (*AILD*, 160).

Her God, in other words, is the personified life force itself and is evidently solely of this world, partaking in all of it, good and bad.

As startling perhaps as any of this is her use of the term "violation." It implies the wrench she feels between her desires for both unusual privacy and extraordinary intimacy. For example, she imagines the intimacy of pregnancy, childbirth, and infant care for Cash as an invasion: "My aloneness had been violated and then made whole again by the violation" (*AILD*, 158). Thus the idea of action daunts as well as attracts her: she says action ("doing") goes "terribly" along the earth, just as she calls blood and living "terrible" (*AILD*, 157). ("Terrible," of course, is used in the original sense, terrifying, as in God's "terrible swift sword" in "The Battle Hymn of the Republic," as well as Faulkner's usage in the phrase "bizarre and terrible.")

But for Addie, ideally, "terrible" physical action that in some way unites her to others allows the "I" to exist at a purely passionate level without the habit or compromise of convention-bound words, which she scorns as thin and harmless. Notice the importance she places on giving birth to Cash and nursing him, having an affair with Whitfield—from which comes one of her two favorite children, the physically active son Jewel—and even beating the schoolchildren in frustration at being blocked from real intimacy with their "blood . . . strange to mine" by the inadequacy of words: "We had had to use one another by words like spiders dangling by their mouths from a beam, swinging and twisting and never touching, and . . . only through the blows of the switch could my blood and their blood flow as one stream" (*AILD*, 158).

By whatever physical means, loving or cruel, rather than endure her acute sense of separation from others, Addie wants her "I" to be in direct contact with others' lives, in a fusion with their "blood" without the mediation of conventions. Conventions are like preestablished social bridges from person to person, the shared implicit assumptions and practices allowing people, after a fashion, to communicate or otherwise act in concert. Addie, almost a romantic mystic, feels that these bridges separate more than they connect, and she wants to sweep them away between herself and others like the flooded river or the wild blood she hears flooding through the land, in order to live directly in this fluid active life. There is a crucial condition, however: to live in this stream, but not blend fluidly. She wants still to retain the proudly private "I" with its specific experience (loss of this distinctiveness, after all, is what words threaten), identity, self-sufficiency. Her stated wish to return to *her* "blood" in the Jefferson burial grounds captures this part of her desire. The doubleness of that longing is captured in the dance her mind does between "of me alone" and "of none and of all" in describing her children: "My children were of me alone, of the wild blood boiling along the earth, of me and of all that lived; of none and of all" (*AILD*, 162).

At a more practical level, clearly, the meaning and reality of all this exists wholly and solely in Addie's mind. Whitfield's subsequent chapter gives no inkling that he either shared her symbolic imaginings or was capable of them. For her, the secrecy necessary for adultery with a minister is the essence of the drama she plays in her head. Secretive to the last, Addie envisions making the lives of others open to her without risking any openness to them. Similarly, the essence of her revenge on Anse is its privacy to herself: "My revenge would be that he would never know I was taking revenge" (*AILD*, 159). Here Addie is a Bundren through and through.

In short, it is a wholly autonomous self that Addie envisions in her vow to herself, "I would be I," an individual free of social arrangements yet profoundly sharing in others' lives at the physical, active level at which all living things share life.

If we were to take Addie's self-portrayal too simply at her own assessment, we would have a novel of individual desire frustrated by social convention. But we are now in a position to appreciate what's wrong when Addie implies that there is a one-way traffic in which one neatly separable entity, desire, is blocked by another entirely different entity, convention. We must add that there is a two-way traffic between the two and that they cannot be so neatly divided from each other. Frustration arises from conflicting desires, and desires themselves both have an impact on conventions and are produced or imprinted by conventions.

Secrecy illustrates this theory of desire-as-convention. All the Bundrens are frustrated by the unspoken family custom, or *convention*, of secrecy embodying the *desire* for self-sufficiency. It's significant that although Addie recognizes and attacks verbal and other conventionality, she fails to see that what she calls "secret and selfish blood" itself embodies a convention. She speaks of it instead as if it were an inevitable fact of life: as natural as blood. She fails to see what the novel stresses—that the secrecy that frustrates her desire for connection with others is a shared and conflicting desire of her own. Her failure to appreciate that secrecy is a desire she shares with others means, to repeat, that she fails to see that it's a *convention*—the customary desire—of her family and society. Her complaint about the inability of words to communicate what is distinctively private to one's experience is a half-truth because it's blind to the mutually shaping interplay of private experience and public language/convention. Her complaint is also blind to the specific disabling impact of secrecy on her family and society. Although Addie feelingly sees more than most, the disabling secrecy she shares creates all this blindness.

Addie is not alone in her desires or needs and frustrations. Darl and Jewel at once come to mind, each jealously yearning toward Addie and each balked in his own way. Dewey Dell also has great hidden fervor, and Vardaman, to a lesser degree, has recently been given a new, anguished access to such powerful feelings.

Part of Dewey Dell's anguish is the frustration of anguish itself. Emotion, denied open expression by the family's customary desire for secrecy, is so bottled up that it is unable to feel itself: "I dont know whether I am worrying or not. Whether I can or not. I dont know whether I can cry or not. I dont know whether I have tried to or not. I feel like a wet seed wild in the hot blind earth" (58). The image of a wild seed in the earth invites partial comparison with Addie's desire to enter fully, sexually into life-giving processes. For her daughter, however, this is an image of an unsayable passion that has become as insentient as the life of a plant: worry unable to know if it is worry, crying unable to know if it is crying. For Dewey Dell, this terrible awakening to the alienation within herself comes from being unable to speak of her unwanted pregnancy by Lafe, a muteness compounded by her mother's death, so she is reduced to saying in her mind to Dr. Peabody that he could do so much for her if he only knew.

For Vardaman, this awakening comes from his mother's death compounded by his family's failure to communicate reassurance and explanation to him—so that he hates Peabody as her murderer, as apparently the one who "came and did it" (AILD, 49). Like Dewey Dell, Vardaman goes to the barn to seek animal comfort. Even more than his sister's seed image, his image of his mother as a fish powerfully indicates, because it is such a grotesque failure of communication, just how much frustrated emotion his family's habits of private feeling have locked up within him. The fish in fact is a traditional image of life and the sharing of life, but this overtone of meaning for readers informed of the non-Christian and Christian associations is ironic, because it is absent for Vardaman and the others.

Matter-of-fact Cash, too, has his revealing moment of shared intensity by the flooded river with Darl, as they contemplate its ravaging natural life. As if under the spell of this embodiment of Addie's terrifying wild blood, they "look at one another with long probing looks, looks that plunge unimpeded through one another's eyes and into the ultimate secret place where for an instant Cash and Darl crouch flagrant and unabashed in all the old terror and the old foreboding, alert and secret and without shame" (AILD,

128). "For an instant" the "ultimate secret place" is shared, but the family desire-as-convention of secrecy triumphs shortly when Cash colludes with the plot to commit Darl to the asylum. So too, it would seem, Darl himself colludes with the secret.

At the novel's end, despite their efforts and the apparent success of their cooperative action in getting Addie's body to the cemetery and supplying themselves with a new Mrs. Bundren and a phonograph as well, none of the Bundrens gets anything remotely matching the capacity of desire and need to which the reader is made witness. Unable to admit one another to ultimate secret places for more than a rare instant, they are left holding the bag of bananas. Even the often ludicrous Anse, who in a sense does get what he wants in teeth and a new wife, earlier manifested a somewhat redeeming capacity for outrage. This potential suggests that in a more significant sense these prizes of Anse's are inadequate even measured against his own (rarely revealed) baffled potentials, however egocentric: "From behind his slack-faced astonishment he muses as though from beyond time, upon the ultimate outrage" (*AILD*, 68), and in such outrage "lurks a wisdom too profound or too inert for even thought" (*AILD*, 45). Finally, so much has the journey taken on a life, and death, of its own that the desire to bury Addie is itself buried at the end, passed over in a few words: "But when we got it filled and covered . . ." (*AILD*, 220).

We can conclude, then, that Addie's frustrated desire is general. Still, considering passive Darl and Anse, one might wonder if there is indeed a general desire or need for action, comparable to Addie's. Only active Jewel seems to fit the description well. It is important to note, however, that what really compels Addie is participation in a larger action than her own individual activity. To her, having sexual relations with Whitfield connects her to all human and natural vital actions, which embody the life force that is God. The key to taking part in this collective life is action, and the means she uses is to act herself.

Others use different means, but the effort to participate in others' actions, if only by acting through them, is general. Darl's way is by imaginative vicarious participation. Jewel's active vigor is exactly what fascinates Darl, who tries to appropriate it, share in it, in his own poetic way, by obsessively perceiving and describing it in the most intensely heightened fashion, so that it becomes surreal, superreal. In heightening Jewel's activity to superreality, Darl adds his own creative activity to his brother's physical force and so takes part in it. Here's a sample: "When Jewel can almost touch him, the horse stands on his hind legs and slashes down at Jewel. Then Jewel is enclosed by a glittering maze of hooves as by an illusion of wings; among them, beneath the upreared chest, he moves with the flashing limberness of a snake. For an instant before the jerk comes onto his arms he sees his whole body earth-free, horizontal, whipping snake-limber, until he finds the horse's nostrils and touches earth again" (*AILD*, 11).

This is part of an exemplary moment in the novel. Darl mercilessly rides Jewel about his attachment to his mother and his dubious parentage, yet seeks to draw power from him by imaginatively engaging Jewel's active force. So too Jewel fights his horse, caresses him, spoils him, and curses him simultaneously, and in general seeks to draw power from this personal totem animal he identifies with through action.

As for lazy Anse, his strategy of life is comparable to Darl's vicariousness because each in his different fashion has others act for him, which is to say each acts through them. But whereas for Darl this is both a desire and a need, for Anse it seems to be simply a need. And whereas Darl—with the disastrous exception of burning the Gillespies' barn—relies on imaginatively satisfying his desire for action through and with others, Anse relies on practical means and ends. There's the rub: Darl the artist figure is relatively harmless in his mental aesthetics, but Anse, though not the novel's villain, epitomizes the villainous potential of conventions.

Anse's way of garnering active power without risking the responsibility for acting himself is to goad others to act for him by manipulating conventions. Anse has spent his lifetime selfishly managing the most banal conventions. He flattens out nearly every emotion except others' shame and guilt, which he arouses and uses. He produces this effect by endlessly repeating clichés designed to attach responsibility and blame to others so that they will act for him—or, in other words, so he can act through them. To claim "we would be beholden to no man" is to manipulate the convention that the Southern farmer is a sturdily independent yeoman, even while flagrantly violating its spirit by piling up dependency upon obligation. "You got no affection nor gentleness for [your mother]" (*AILD*, 18), he accuses the impatient Jewel after wearing Jewel's patience down by a protracted display of "undecision," as Anse calls it—and before dragging the mother's body across the land in his determination to get to Jefferson.

Here is Anse again in typical "inactive" action, wanting to use Tull's mule to help cross the river: "I aint asking it of you . . . I can always do for me and mine. I aint asking you to risk your mule. It aint your dead; I am not blaming you" (*AILD*, 124). I'm not asking and not blaming, he repeats as he asks and blames his way into a power over others that they notice disbelievingly but cannot escape. Jewel even gives up his beloved horse after Anse has traded it away without consulting him. Jewel yields his horse unwillingly, but like everyone else he finally capitulates to Anse's relentless nagging, shaming, and blaming.

This novel, then, represents collective action in fragmented potentials and forms. Jewel, Darl, Anse, and Addie in particular represent extreme types. Jewel suggests the extreme physical, inarticulate face of collective action, by main force helping the journey to completion but unable to extend himself beyond obsessive paired relationships, with his mother or with his horse. Darl shows the extreme private face of collective action. His is an imaginative form consisting of secretly identifying with some active other person or group by a private, subjective re-creation of this other. Anse is the extreme public face. His is an instrumental form consisting of external manipulation of more active others by operating conventions, not for a truly common practical goal but only for the weak imitation of cooperative action that is the burial journey.

Addie combines all these extremes. In Jewel's direct, physical way she goes after what she wants. "So I took Anse," she says (*AILD*, 157), and later, apparently, she takes Whitfield also. As Darl poetically remodels Jewel, she surreally envisions Whitfield through an immensely heightened action in which she imaginatively participates. In Anse's instrumental fashion, she acts vicariously also by manipulating Anse, and her family with him, into a journey in which they act for her and she acts through them. Yet the divergence between her aim of revenge and Anse's "triumphant" aims epitomizes the fracturing of genuinely common purpose.

As extreme forms, these faces of collective action make up the larger travesty that is the journey. We saw earlier that these extremes meet and intertwine, reinforcing each other in their very conflict, because extreme privacy in the form of self-sufficiency is one of the major publicly acknowledged conventions Anse knows so well how to maneuver. This point suggests, again, that private desire and public convention cannot be neatly, sweepingly opposed to each other. When they are in conflict, it is as a dialectical pair. That is, in their very conflict they simultaneously influence and feed each other.

The plot of the perilous family journey in its most ideal moments of cooperation—as, for example, at times during the dangerous river crossing—shows another desire or need than that of self-sufficiency. If this compulsion were a title, it would say, not *As I Lay Dying*, but *As We Acted Together for a Shared Purpose*. The book's actual title implies that desire or need only by naming its usual, actual fragmenting and thwarting in the Bundrens' social world. Instead of "we" there is usually a lonely "I," and instead of a sufficiently vital collective action there is something in between, neither fully life nor death, neither fully collective nor noncollective.

As noted before, if we were to see the novel only in terms of Addie's vow, "I would be I," the narrative's central conflict would simply be that between the passionate, rootless romantic individual and the shackles of social convention. This perspective is useful because it emphasizes certain significant features of the novel that are in the tradition of romantic individualism, very much alive in the twenties and continuing to our own time.

But *As I Lay Dying* gives its own distinctive turn to this standard story that Western culture has been telling itself often for at least two centuries. This is a "thirties" turn toward a preoccupation with collective action and with all that diverts people from the more promising forms of cooperation into poor imitations like the Bundrens' journey.

# 6

## *Making the Invisible Visible*

### WORN SO IN FADING PRECISION

The people of this novel are far from being embodiments of "Lost Generation" rootlessness because, although their community is defective, they are still very much rooted in social conventions even as they may struggle in their grasp. As a result, Faulkner's critique of convention works not at the surfaces of his characters but close to the bone. The novel's tonal interplay challenges the reader's critical imagination to work at the same point.

The predominant tone of the novel may well strike us as humorously grotesque in the beginning because we see only glimpses of what the triumph of the stale conventionality of an Anse might really mean. More important, readers are likely to find Anse's behavior so transparently hypocritical and petty, like Cora Tull's, that, however contemptible, he seems ludicrously harmless. So it seems to Addie, who equates him with words and imagines that they go quickly and harmlessly into the air. (Neither Anse nor words are harmless.) It's easy to share the humor of his neighbors as they shake their heads in exasperated fatalism at the way Anse gets everyone to do what he wants. It's even easier to underestimate Anse also because Faulkner takes pains to display a comparable eccentricity or grotesquery in Anse's family and his world.

At first, Cash's behavior and his narration seem to present him simply as his father's son: Cash's noisy construction of Addie's coffin right before her eyes; his amusing numbered list of reasons why he beveled the boards—item 6, ludicrously, is the single word, "Except" (*AILD*, 73); his reply to a question about how far he fell off the church roof, "Twenty-eight foot, four and a half inches, about" (*AILD*, 80)—taken together, all this and more adds up to a slightly wicked caricature of someone as humorless as Anse but as entertainingly straightforward and overprecise as Anse is devious and sloppy. Faulkner's placement of Vardaman's conclusion that his mother is a fish immediately after the deadpan humor of Cash's list gives Vardaman's grotesque statement, despite its pathetic potentials, a similarly wickedly comic undertone, since it seems a continuation of Cash's earnest, unconsciously droll explanation.

Even more wickedly comic is Faulkner's caricature of a partial analogue to Anse, Cora, through her own narration and through the eyes of her long-suffering but fatalistically admiring husband, Vernon Tull. In a more genial vein, there is the general humor of the vernacular, like "I be durn if . . ." or "I be dogged if . . ." as well as the characters' quite conscious humor such as the joking about how many children Uncle Billy has fathered and how the Lord too has to help Anse: "I reckon He's like everybody else around here," Uncle Billy says. "He's done it so long now He cant quit" (*AILD*, 79).

In fact, readers might go beyond detached amusement at Anse and the general eccentricity and grotesquery to feel detachment, period, toward all the Bundrens. We have no secure frame of narrative reference and no narrator easy to identify with. And how extraordinary are the constantly changed perspectives—in a brief novel amounting to about 240 small pages in our edition, we have 59 short chapters presented by 15 alternating speakers. So it's not difficult for readers to view the family from a certain distance.

This distance may increase to the point of complete detachment because of one powerful, widespread convention: that fictions should have protagonists with whom many people can identify, to a large degree if not entirely. Many fictions—books, movies, music, television—rely heavily on this habit, which is supposedly suited to what's called the general public, or perhaps to those times when all of us wish to do little but consume easily consumed entertainment. Nevertheless, what are most traditionally esteemed as masterworks, from Homer through Dickens, often draw upon the convention too.

Much of what is called high modernist literature, however, challenges this convention of easy identification by having protagonists with whom fewer people can identify and who may be uncomfortable to live with even if we identify with them to a degree. Addie and Darl are cut from such modernist cloth: intelligent and sensitive, but unconventional, not easy to understand, and manifesting a streak of cruelty. Addie at one point derives a perverse satisfaction from beating her students, and Darl mercilessly mocks Jewel about his parentage and about Addie's death and putrefaction. Some readers have proposed the character of Cash as providing a sympathetic protagonist, or at least viewpoint, but others have made strong arguments pointing out the difficulties of this position. A similar, though rarer, case has been presented for Jewel, but the difficulties here are, if anything, greater. At any rate, the point is that identification with one or more characters has proven to be far from easy.

This novel challenges the convention of easy identification with the protagonist more than most modernist works because of its additional violations of conservative reading habits. Especially for present-day urban readers, and particularly non-Southerners, all these twenties rural characters and their way of life may seem so utterly foreign to familiar habits and conventions that they appear as, at best, mildly interesting curiosities. If readers accept literary and nonliterary conventions, and especially if they unthinkingly regard these conventions as something natural and universally applicable, which they aren't, readers are even more unlikely to grasp the full implications of the devastation-by-conventionality that Anse represents in only apparently harmless comic form.

The many readers who have admired this novel, however, often develop a concern for the characters that complicates and, though perhaps gradually, predominates over the forms of detachment just described, but without necessarily eliminating a certain critical distance. The earlier account of readers' reactions to the characters has assumed such a mixed reaction. As we read through and around Anse's foolishness and the other characters' oddities, there are, for these readers, troubling, eloquent disclosures of the family's frustrated emotion that accumulate in the narratives by the Bundren children, especially the imaginative though disturbed Darl. But the novel's potential for having impact as a serious work becomes most powerful only two-thirds of the way through, when Addie's chapter gives us our first sufficient yardstick, a "before and after" sketch of her calamitous marriage, to measure what the past and future petty triumph of Anse has cost and will cost, the toll on life that his kind of parasitism takes.

Addie's section encapsulates the course of her life by contrasting her youthful tormented longing with all the barriers to the fulfillment of longing. Her father had told her that "the reason for living was to get ready to stay dead a long time" (*AILD*, 155), and she sharply feels the flow of brief individual life bounded by the infinitude, the "long time," of death. So frustrated is her longing for the transient vitality all around her, yet closed to her, that she cannot bear the thought that her students carry it within them as a "secret and selfish life," and she masochistically beats them. Her cruelty is masochistic because "when the switch fell I could feel it upon my flesh; when it welted and ridged it was my blood that ran" (*AILD*, 155).

Addie believes that she has entered into others' lives in this violent action by marking their blood with her own "for ever and ever" (*AILD*, 155), but here and throughout, her goal of actively sharing life's passionate vitality is frustrated by its very means of even momentary achievement. This frustration is shown by the increasingly desperate measures she takes and the continuing masochistic or self-defeating nature of these measures. Addie, as we saw, distrusts words as the medium for communion with others' collective life because they epitomize the emptiness of conventions.

She instead trusts in bodily action, but each of her living endeavors is only momentarily satisfying, and her claim to have found lasting peace finally in Jewel's birth is belied by the continued longing, frustration, and outrage that mark her narration. It is also contradicted by the flashback a few pages earlier that showed her mixed pride and pain in being superseded in Jewel's affections by his hard-earned horse. Her planned burial journey is the capstone of her life lived in anticipation of death.

Three points can be noted briefly here. First, the family's way of accomplishing her goal of burial mocks the very object of Addie's devotion, bodily action with others, by turning her and her journey into a public spectacle of decomposing flesh. Second, Addie's life is warped and worn by convention not only directly, through her frustrating association with those like Anse and Cora, but also indirectly, by the way she reacts against convention. In scorning words as an inadequate conventional medium for a communion with intense life, she goes to the opposite extreme of making a tragically limited fetish of physical action. And third, readers have often found that the novel invites considerable sympathy for her and her defeat in a number of ways. Even in her cruelty and her mistakes, to many readers her passion rings with an authenticity and depth that is attractive, compared to Anse's false, unimaginative life. Faulkner makes it additionally attractive by giving this skeptic of words, Addie, dazzling language to make her case and by putting her monologue between those of the self-righteous hypocrites, Cora and Whitfield, so that Addie's impatience with such cant appears more attractive by contrast.

More generally, Faulkner amplifies Addie's predicament as a frustrated, strong-willed, imaginative woman by emphasizing the difficult life of women in this rural patriarchy. Early in the novel, Tull says, "It's a hard life on women, for a fact" (*AILD*, 25), and the idea is repeated at intervals (*AILD*, 21, 24, 41, 47, 173, and 187). In fact, when first Rachel Samson and then Lula Armstid call Anse's behavior towards Addie's body outrageous, they suggest that it typifies a general mistreatment, as in Rachel's truncated protest: "I just wish that you and him and all the men in the world that torture us alive and flout us dead, dragging us up and down the country—" (*AILD*, 103).

In these ways and others, the novel prompts us to assess the high cost of the conventionality that Anse represents. Having balanced this cost, the novel travels the last section of its tightrope between the bizarre and the terrible by returning at the end to the grotesque humor of Anse's transparent ruses and dodges.

But as a result, things that were before just bizarre can now be seen also as subtly terrible. Anse's pettiness is far from negligible. It was our mistake to think it was, as apparently it was Addie's when, as she says, she "took Anse" by marrying him. By initially presenting Anse as harmless, as if he were in fact like a passive entity to be "taken," and by delaying Addie's own account, the novel works to maneuver us as readers into Addie's error of underestimating Anse so we can share her experience of frustrated desire more acutely than we could have otherwise. The episode of Darl's incarceration near the novel's end helps us to see what Anse is capable of doing and refreshes our memory of Addie's parallel error in rejecting Darl at birth.

We can say without exaggeration that petty conventionality, though belied by Anse's feckless appearance, is the most dangerous force in the book. It is far more deadly than the fire and flood that the family has survived, more powerful even than Addie with her wild desire for life lived at maximum pitch. Part of its danger is precisely that pettiness, exemplified in its devotee, Anse, *still* looks so innocuously foolish at the end, "hang-dog and proud too" with new teeth and a new, duck-shaped wife (*AILD*, 241).

Darl senses that convention works by attrition to wear down all that makes for real life: "When something is new and hard and bright, there ought to be something a little better for it than just being safe, since the safe things are just the things that folks have been doing so long they have worn the edges off" (*AILD*, 117).

Anse's pettiness, then, does more than wear people's patience thin. It evokes the daily minute abrasion of self-serving, inert conventions simplifying everything to blame, shame, and guilt and thus wearing away at passionate vitality until it finally grinds the more aspiring life down. Just about everyone in the novel repeats conventional phrases, but Anse's repetitions are the most important and striking because coupled with his refusal to take responsibility for acting or deciding at crucial moments are his obvious hypocrisy and manipulation. His conventionality is shown as monstrous because it's combined with comically—and tragically—unconventional means and ends.

From the first page of the book the effects of slow wearing appear, beginning with the path Darl walks across the field, "worn so by feet in fading precision," and the cotton house leaning in "shimmering dilapidation in the sunlight" whose low but unrelenting impact has gradually helped to break it down (*AILD*, 3). Anse's power of attrition is the counterpart to the repeated human actions that wore the path across the field, and it also parallels the warping and eroding force of passing time, which, though not by itself, wears and misshapes his wife's hands to gnarled roots on her deathbed (*AILD*, 13). Robbing Cash, Jewel, and finally Dewey Dell, impassively allowing Darl to be taken away to the asylum, and all the while mouthing his self-serving clichés about loyalty to parents and his hard lot, Anse at last gets his teeth and a replacement wife to consume as he has consumed Addie. To use one of Vardaman's inadvertently apt phrases, this duck-shaped woman, like Addie, will be metaphorically "cooked and et" (*AILD*, 52). She too will be devoured slowly by Anse, simply by his being Anse, though perhaps more swiftly than Addie was, since the substitute wife's openly defiant aggressiveness and comic appearance suggest that she is a mere caricature of the secretly aggressive first Mrs. Bundren.

Coming to this final scene, we encounter the old joke again about Anse's being the unlikely one who somehow comes out on top. The novel's humor here becomes, fittingly, as exasperating as Anse. We can see him and his blinking eyes now with unblinkered eyes of our own. We can now grasp better the accumulating force of mere unremitting banality in Anse's final meanness and triumph. We know, or should know, that the spectacular flood and fire the family has faced are not the really triumphant destructive powers. And yet, we cannot fully feel about Anse's nearly invisible abrasive force the rage, awe, fear, and pity such a destructive power should evoke, and which we might well experience in witnessing the dramatic effects of flood and fire or some obviously monstrous human villain. Like Anse at the beginning, we somehow "cant seem to get no heart" into these feelings (*AILD*, 34), even as we judge that we should have them and even want to have them.

This is, after all, just Anse being Anse; and for all that the novel has led me to intuit about what he represents, he as an individual still looks harmless and inept. This is especially so as Cash, the final narrator, in his equable, convention-mindful voice works to smooth away the violent attack on Darl while Anse doesn't even turn a hair. Again, the disparity—between, on the one hand, the annihilating power of manipulative conventionality that Anse best represents and, on the other, "Anse himself"—is too great. He is, precisely, too pettily conventional; his protective coloration is the best there is, the "perverse ubiquity" (*AILD*, 48) of the cliché.

All this is dismaying and exasperatingly humorous. And it is wonderfully right. For what this ending, like the novel as a whole, does is create the opportunity for readers to grasp almost viscerally what the novel is about. The readers' emotional bind parallels the experience of the characters. For the last time and superlatively, the sequence of reading events invites us to experience for ourselves two different sensations. There is an arousal of emotion—

say, dismay and resentment—at the fact that the Bundrens have been thwarted in the full life they need, and simultaneously the frustration, the flattening out, of emotion. Our feeling is thwarted, fittingly, by none other than Anse, because he is just too petty for us to focus these emotions against. We are in Addie's position, our emotional life aroused and provoked by the threat to it that Anse's pettiness represents and yet also in some measure frustrated in its expression, frustrated by the very pettiness of Anse "himself." Anse too is warped and worn by it as surely as his shoulders are humped by his buzzard-like posture, as surely as he makes even astonishment banal: "He looks around, blinking, in that surprised way, like he had wore hisself down being surprised and was even surprised at that" (*AILD*, 28).

To put the matter another way, we are in the position of Rachel Samson and Lula Armstid, except that we feel, as they may not, the distracting yet fitting absurdity that lurks in our impulse to protest at Anse and his works: it's a outrage. By repeatedly giving us pause for a variety of reasons, the book prompts us to think beyond Anse.

## PROBLEM: HEROIC PASSIONS VERSUS "NORMAL" VEXATIONS

A few years before this novel was published, T. S. Eliot had written in "The Hollow Men" that the way the world ends is not with a bang but a whimper. Exactly so here. As readers have often remarked, Darl gives us images of the bang, a vision of apocalyptic ruin. In his eyes, when they come to the flooded river, it is "as though we had reached the place where the motion of the wasted world accelerates just before the final precipice" (*AILD*, 133).

Darl fashions such images with the gifts of a lyric poet both fearing and desiring an explosive, poetically grand end to things. He does so exactly because he understands something akin to what Eliot calls the whimper: that a slower disintegrating force is at work around him, symbolized by the process of decomposition within Addie's coffin and the patiently circling buzzards, which Darl with ominous simplicity calls "they." An important, highly compressed statement by Darl implies that, in a more conventional form, every-one shares his desire for a dramatic end, to make death a significant one-time event rather than a wearing repetitive process of social life itself: "How do our lives ravel out into the no-wind, no-sound, the weary gestures wearily recapitulant: echoes of old compulsions with no-hand on no-strings: in sunset we fall into furious attitudes, dead gestures of dolls" (*AILD*, 191).

Darl contrasts here an actual inglorious lifetime of ravelling with the energetic dramas and rituals—what he sardonically calls "furious attitudes" and "dead gestures"— accompanying the event of physical death, "sunset." In this fatalistic frame of mind, he thinks that, if conventions inevitably wear the edges off all that's "new and hard and bright," it would be best if one could simply "ravel out in time" (*AILD*, 193) instead of going through one more set of conventions, such "dead gestures of dolls" as the burial ritual in which he finds himself participating.

Faulkner uses his Darl-like lyric gift as a writer to warn that even in this journey of rural folk the world's real apocalypse is indeed at work. But since it looks like anything but an apocalypse, Faulkner combines the compressed poetic images with the cumulative effects of narrative to create the reading experience of a destructive force working untiringly over long stretches of time. It's as if in his cataclysmic visions Darl is trying to conjure up a great antagonist in a single, tangible form so it can be clearly seen and defied: "The thick dark current . . . talks up to us in a murmur become ceaseless and myriad, the yellow surface dimpled monstrously . . . as though just beneath the surface something huge and alive waked for a moment of lazy alertness out of and ii.to light slumber again" (*AILD*, 127). But the all too banal melting away of life cannot be coerced into making an explosive "lyric" display of itself. Its slow momentum is like the force of vermin, of termites and ants (say Anse's name), invisibly devouring what appear to be mightier things than themselves.

Yet though Faulkner makes such helpful analogies from nature, they can be seen as mainly analogies. The apocalypse that Faulkner is primarily interested in is not a natural but a social attrition. The power of social, conventional forces is what puts the Bundrens at risk of the natural forces, bringing them to dare the dangerous river when three sane alternatives exist. The microscopic Anse-like forces of inertial convention support a minimal but long-enduring existence. As Anse does with Addie, they not only wear away but parasitically live off other lives, "living off them that sweats" (*AILD*, 97). As these words of Anse's demonstrate, it was not a natural event but a particular set of socioeconomic arrangements that warped his feet because his childhood shoes were homemade and that gnarled Addie's hands by making farm work so crushing on women. Like the nature analogues, the novel's bizarre and terrible events, its images, and its characterization strive to unmask these "normal" things in all their real grotesquery. For, again, the trite normality of their dissolving power is also their protective coloration—nothing escapes real notice like the profoundly commonplace things.

Faulkner is known for his fireworks as a stylist, and this novel lavishes visceral images on the Bundrens. But he often uses these stylistic fireworks to help him get at something the opposite of pyrotechnical, which is the despair and the lure of many novelists, as well as humbler everyday storytellers. The microprocesses of social life and death can be as hard to focus as grass growing and dying. But in them, Faulkner suggests, the life of life and the death of death work themselves out every day.

The Faulkner we are discussing here is the Faulkner who created Anse Bundren as a finally ominous clown patched together of maddeningly repeated clichés—Anse, a man whose ideal of a slow vegetable life is summed up in his comically solemn complaint that roads, tempting people to move about, are contrary to human nature because human beings are vertical like trees and thus are meant to be stationary (*AILD*, 31). Anse's appeal here to the laws of nature to support what is really a humanly created interpretation of his own is typical. Conventions, too, usually present themselves as if they were laws as natural as trees and so to be taken for granted, when actually they are humanly created and must be maintained or changed by human action.

This is also the Faulkner who, in tones of high seriousness and in exalted language, had recently presented Mr. Compson in *The Sound and the Fury* teaching his son Quentin that a noble passion is not dramatically defeated but just slowly ground into nothing: "Christ was not crucified: he was worn away by a minute clicking of little [clock] wheels."[8] Critics have often commented on the similarities between Quentin Compson and Darl Bundren. They are especially alike in their hunger for a cataclysm in preference to feeling their lives being daily ground away. Darl and Quentin are like a writer who wants to create a heroic literature of tragic defeats and so wants an antagonist of correspondingly heroic proportions, yet who sees that the tepid antagonist who brings down their world is utterly incongruous with the large passions it stifles and the "new and hard and bright" edges it wears away.

What do you do as a writer when the real villain facing your passionate hero or heroine is mere deadly, "normal" convention? The problem is not so much capturing the drab, wearing everyday-ness of things. Some purely realistic fiction does this admirably. But usually it does so at the price of having protagonists who are, so to speak, much the same size as the "normally" petty world that defeats them; otherwise, the fictional illusion we call realism is destroyed. At the other extreme, a writer can show a passionate intelligence such as that of Oedipus being brought down by such massive opponents as fate and his own courageous determination to know the truth. What is extremely difficult to do artistically, however, is to combine in one work the passionate soul—the Oedipus or Medea type—with a mundane attrition that thwarts it.

It will be helpful at this point to see how other fictions handle this or a similar difficulty. Some fictions are satisfying emotionally, if not intellectually, because they simplify all the things that frustrate our desires (for justice, love, understanding, and so on) by personifying this opposition in a tangible, obviously evil or misguided villain. Just as important, we are never in doubt that this figure adequately fills the role of antagonist, such that when the villain is either destroyed or even triumphs, there is a welcome sense of something resolved, one way or another.

Even in works that complicate this approach, as when the protagonist's own character plays a part in her or his downfall, this emotional demand is often satisfied by the creation of a worthy antagonist. Oedipus has the Fates and Othello has Iago. From the standpoint of most classical tragedy, Addie, with her larger-than-life ambitions, "deserved" a grand antagonist to defeat her, even though her character is inseparable from her "fate."

When the mighty are defeated by ordinariness, like a lion by quicksand, what do you do then?

One strategy you can use is to alternate tragically serious suffering with switches in tone that prevent tragic momentum from developing. The novel's ending recapitulates this technique climactically. The novel's mixed tone works throughout to frustrate tragic catharsis, the release of "serious" emotions, in order to involve readers in the Bundrens' frustration. So, too, high passions are locked into eloquent literary language in the characters' minds, in a rhetoric that cannot be expressed and shared within the conventions of the characters' world. This device creates a tragic tone, while embodying the blockage by ruinous family and social conventions. In other words, if the situation being depicted precludes a fully tragic treatment according to traditional conventions of tragedy, Faulkner makes a point of this very preclusion to reinforce his critique of conventions.

Another thing you can do, if you are Faulkner, is to use the art of caricature. Early attracted to the possibility of a career as a visual artist, Faulkner was a talented sketcher who used distortion to create selective emphasis. Darl at one point describes Anse as having "a face carved by a savage caricaturist" (*AILD*, 69). Throughout his novel, Faulkner is the caricaturist, simplifying and selectively enlarging features of psychology and behavior to create one grotesque portrayal after another. Anse is only the most evident example of these caricatures designed to show the abnormality in what we take to be normal. It's as if Faulkner were saying, "Look, these are the destructive forces at work in the conventions we take for granted, the deadly microscopic features in our life."

Faulkner creates cartoons as tragedy, tragedy as cartoons. It is indeed "savage" for a caricaturist to do this, for as creatures of habit we may well find it discomforting or unnerving to look askance at the habits whose creatures we are.

Faulkner's third general device for making visible what is taken for granted is to emphasize the very conventions of reading that we usually take for granted, so in this respect too we become entangled in the usually invisible conventions of our lives.

## READING CONVENTIONS AS SOCIAL CONVENTIONS

Our discussion has come back to one point repeatedly: *As I Lay Dying* is a bizarre book. This is a novel in which one of the main characters, Addie, says of her husband Anse that he doesn't know that he is dead yet. Far more bizarre is that as we encounter this revealing statement, two-thirds through the novel, we are reading the words of a character who herself has died several days (and many pages) earlier, whose corpse has already begun to stink. She now makes a sudden appearance for the first time as a narrator, with a living intensity that comes equally as a revelation and a shock, to turn the tables on us by saying that it is Anse who is really dead but doesn't know it and to imply that it is she with her intense hunger for life who is really still alive in some sense. Yet again, having apparently at last reentered the novel to narrate it, as the title leads us to expect that she would have done from the first page, Addie promptly disappears from the role of narrator after these few cryptic pages. Nothing in our reading of the novel is the same after we hear this startling voice issue from some unlocatable point in time and space and then vanish.

The surprise tactics Faulkner uses here are not at all unusual in this book. Reading is repeatedly thrown off balance by such abrupt arousals and denials of our expectations for making sense of what we read. These expectations embody story-reading conventions that we have learned and practiced to the point that they seem natural, as if inborn instead of learned, an invisible part of our very selves. They are, obviously, not natural at all. "Real life" does not, as books do, have a convention of supplying quotation marks when people speak, or organizing their activities into chapters with titles or numbers, or allowing us to look directly into their minds—nor, to turn to movies or television, does "real life" provide background music and lighting effects tailored to heighten the action and mood. All these techniques and many others are means of fictional representation, basic devices for getting a story told by creating an illusion of "real life" for an audience which has learned to accept that these devices spell out "real life." Even the most realist fictions in any medium employ many such conventions, both "realistic" and "nonrealistic" ones, which we usually ignore *as* conventions. Nor, as a rule, are we meant to pay attention to them, since this would hurt the illusion of directly perceived reality that realist fictions strive to convey. Clearly, Faulkner is partly playing by different rules, or conventions.

In important respects this is not a work of literary realism, despite its pungent elements of realism like the rural dialogue. But then, if we look at most of the stories told in the world as far back as we can, they ignore realism's rules-that-we-usually-don't-notice-as-rules. In mixing conventions, Faulkner's text encourages its readers to be more aware of conventions as we apply them in the act of reading. Part of the means Faulkner uses to dramatize the usually invisible power of conventions in our lives is juggling novelistic conventions so that they are brought from the background to the foreground of our attention.

A key convention of realistic fiction requires narrative consistency in tone and style. The convention is that a narrator who sounds like a countrified Huck Finn in one sentence should avoid sounding like an aristocratic, educated Prince Hamlet in another. And, usually, there should be an overall narrating consciousness, a mind viewing the novel's events from one perspective. With this novel, however, we must adjust acrobatically to a variety of first-person narrators, styles, and tones following each other in rapid succession. We remarked, for instance, that Addie, Darl, Dewey Dell, and even young Vardaman sometimes speak within their minds in an ornate literary style literally incredible for such rural speakers, clashing with the rural-Mississippi way they talk to each other. Vardaman would not say aloud to anyone what he describes in his interior monologue: "It is as though the dark were resolving [the horse] out of his integrity, into an unrelated scattering of components . . . an illusion of a co-ordinated whole" (*AILD*, 52; see also, e.g., 10–11, 58). Not only that, but as we see when Darl clairvoyantly describes his mother's death although he is physically absent (*AILD*, 43–48), even when the novel supplies us with an "all-knowing" perspective, it makes it bizarre rather than conventional.

Sometimes the novel refers to incidents or characters that have not appeared yet in the chronological events. For example, Cora and Vernon Tull refer to events of the Bundren journey *before they have occurred* (*AILD*, 20, 82), and near the end Cash as narrator refers to "Mrs. Bundren" before Anse even meets his new wife. One may account for these shifts with the view that the time of narration in the novel is later than the time of the events, and that the changes from past to present tense (as in Tull's description of the river crossing) express degrees of psychological involvement or distancing. Even so, the most consistent feature of these devices is their remarkable unconventionality, and the unexplained abrupt jumps in time still disrupt, and call attention to, the convention that people are supposed to be as unambiguously located within one time frame as within one voice.

People who are alive but dead, or dead but alive, a crowd of "I's" speaking to us in sometimes improbable literary voices from rapidly changing perspectives that seemingly violate the laws of space and time—these are some of the related turbulences created in realistic storytelling conventions, the very conventions, in fact, that the novel follows so expertly at other times.

More than just literary conventions are at stake here. Conventions of storytelling correspond to conventions of living—to conventional beliefs and habits of cultures, including economic, political, and religious ones. For example, consistently realistic dialogue corresponds to a cultural assumption about consistent identity. The belief that characters should speak in a uniform style is part of a dominant cultural belief that individual identity is pretty much whole, self-consistent, and separable from other forms of identity. As such, it provides the model for identity and must be represented and respected above all. The assumption goes that the individual voice is the sign of this paradigm identity, and as identity is supposedly self-consistent and has clear boundaries between the "I" and the "not-I," so should voice. Thus the outrages of story conventions in *As I Lay Dying* can create moments of reading vertigo related to one of the novel's key questions: where does the "I" begin and end? The novel's disorienting of the boundaries of individual and group identities is made significant by its emphasis on the collective, interactive nature of feelings and actions.

These violations of literary realism, with its cultural convention of the individual as the ultimate model, take on meaning within the different, social model of existence such as the one that Peabody brings into focus. In this inclusive context, the individual's life and death and his or her sharply limited experience of space and time are but phases passing into the ongoing collective experience of the group, which stretches across space and time. Taking this view allows us to make sense of the novel's revolt against the restrictions of the individualist convention, as part of the critique of an excessive cultural individualism.

This view as well, however, has to be considered in the light of our discussion so far, which indicates that the novel's voices do not securely make up some collective whole. On the contrary, to borrow Vardaman's description of the horse, what we encounter in every feature of this novel is better understood as a social entity resolved into scattered components. Like the collective action of the journey, they represent the illusion, or the shaky periodic achievement, of a coordinated whole. The narrative voices imply a fragmented collective like the divergent but overlapping motives and actions of the novel, and like the paradoxical community bound by an ethos of secretive privacy.

No clearly consistent collective voice speaks, any more than consistently individual voices do. The novel, setting out to roil narrative-cultural conventions and thus bring them to our notice, shuttles in between the individual and the collective voice. It might be said that the novel puts readers in the position of earning, if they can and will, the perspective of collective action by going through the narrative's revolt against conventional realism and its corresponding individual-centered assumptions.

In all this the novel moves parallel to the more despairing self-inquisition Darl practices as he feels that his life is diffusely scattered among others and so questions not only his identity but even his existence. We cannot comfort ourselves that Darl goes mad and so his perceptions lack any general significance. Darl's frequent self-doubt helps the whole novel to insinuate its discomforting focus on the transitory, fluid nature of the "I," as in his rendering of the melting power of the flooded river: "As if the clotting which is you had dissolved into the myriad original motion" (*AILD*, 149–50). One of Darl's, and the novel's, favorite concepts, "dissolves," appears here. Another of the novel's favorites is "shape" as both verb and noun. These ideas work to similar effect to remind us often that, from a broad perspective like that Darl takes in the last quotation, boundaries of identity are but passing forms and phases, "clottings" being dissolved and reshaped anew within the vast "original motion" of social and natural existence.

In spotlighting the microscopic processes of social life and death, the novel extends this strategy down to the level of the details of language. For example, the manuscript of the text shows that Faulkner worked to blur the clean lines of individual identity at the level of pronoun references, often substituting *unclear* pronouns for the names or clear references of the first draft.

All these elements in conjunction with the title insinuate that the "I" in *As I Lay Dying* is a free-floating label that can adhere temporarily not only to Addie but to any number of first persons singular. Recurrent images of entities that lose their accustomed fixity and float free make "free-floating" the appropriate description for identities: for example, in death Addie's face "seems to float detached" (*AILD*, 46); to Vardaman's perception Jewel's horse dissolves and "float[s] upon the dark in fading solution" (*AILD*, 52); and at the flooded river, it is as if the road has "soaked free of earth and floated upward" (*AILD*, 129). Similarly, Dewey Dell says of her experience of awaking "with a black void rushing under me" that "That was when I died that time" (*AILD*, 107).

Appropriately to such a novel, the title is like one of those puzzles that asks, "What's wrong with this picture?" Subtly asking who, and where, the "I" could possibly be, the provocative "I" on the book's cover is ready to come unstuck. One way of saying what's "wrong" with the title is that (as with Dewey Dell's statement just quoted) "I" cannot literally tell a story about my life after my death, nor can "I" tell my death.

In the context of the novel, the title means that as an individual you cannot tell the whole story of your own life. First, it is impossible to narrate an important, quasi-conclusive episode, your physical death, an event which, many have traditionally thought, can put your whole life into revealing perspective. Because you cannot complete your story, you cannot tell the whole story.

Others must and will complete the story of our lives by telling about our deaths, just as Addie's death, funeral, and burial are taken under control by others' interpretations. These interpretations derive from their divergent individual desires, all permeated by the shared family desire for secrecy and self-sufficiency as well as the "terrible" lure of collective action. This takeover of the individual's life story occurs no matter how much a strong-willed woman like Addie has tried to manage her own death by extracting a promise from her husband that he will bury her in her family's plot and no matter how much he and others cite her wishes or needs in order to justify themselves. But neither is her wish a negligible feature of this other family plot. Her individual manipulation of the social convention of the "dying wish" is the initiator and exemplar of the journey.

What is true of our deaths also holds for other important parts of our lives—we cannot give first-hand accounts of our births and the important formative period of infancy, for example. Darl and Cash clairvoyantly share a memory of Jewel as a sickly infant on a pillow that Jewel presumably could not recount on his own (*AILD*, 130). In an extended sense this limitation is true for our lives as a whole. Lacking absolute detachment from others as well as ourselves and significantly lacking self-knowledge, we cannot narrate our lives as a whole, but others will and must fill them out. First of all, the many interpretive "ministories" others tell about us in the form of comments, discussions, and gossip have a great cumulative impact on our experiences with others. Second, in fact this continuous discourse concerning us influences our own self-opinion, the account we give of ourselves *to* ourselves and to others, and thus shapes our actions and our identities. This is what Cash grasps when Darl is committed to the insane asylum: "Sometimes I think it aint none of us pure crazy and aint none of us pure sane until the balance of us talks him that-a-way" (*AILD*, 216).

This shaping force is especially vivid within a family. In the daily casual discourse of families, children's personalities are formed as their elders and siblings see them, talk to them, and talk about them, and as children learn to form their own ongoing or anecdotal stories in reply to this context. As we saw, Darl, devastated by his mother's rejection, ceaselessly notes everything Jewel does. Darl's often elaborately stylized descriptions seem designed to appropriate and create Jewel anew as Darl's own, aesthetic creation instead of the product of Addie's favoritism.

In its formative (and destructive) power, culture is like both an extended family and an artist far more powerful than Darl. Unfortunately for Darl, when he is consigned to the insane asylum, culture completes the work of undermining his identity that was begun by Addie. Although Cash is favored by Addie and is as comparatively solid in himself as in his narration, he understands in his own way the collective impact of others' stories on our lives, "talking" us into being what we are.

The general point is that the "I" is deeply involved with others in an intricate dialogue of mutually dependent stories that help to talk the "I" into whatever he or she is. Correspondingly, we perceive Addie's startling story about herself within the cross-hatching of others' accounts of her, and vice versa. Most of these accounts are given by family members whose identities she has directly helped to shape. Like Addie, all exist as shaped and shaping forces within a web of stories that everyone constantly weaves and rends, adding a bit here and unsticking a bit there. So, for example, although I conventionally speak of "the" story of "my" life, I cannot, by myself, at any moment complete either the many stories of my life or the very life that these stories recount.

Beginning with the dangling phrase that is the title, Faulkner fills his novel with incomplete statements, ellipses of both phrasing and thought, and interruptions of both conversation and narrative ("The Lord giveth," "If they want it to tote and ride on a balance, they will have," and so on). These accentuate the necessity for narrative completion by someone other than the speaker, as well as the clash and tangle of others' stories running across not only our talk but also our mental soliloquies, making them dialogues, so to speak, whether they want to be or not. The brevity of the chapters increases the effect of the multitude of daily, anecdotal, miniature narratives that crisscross and accumulate to add up to our lives.

We can generalize, then, from the family level to the level of culture. What we call our culture is the large warehouse (or ongoing theater) of shared general explanatory stories that form our existence. Unless we as individuals can draw upon this general store to coproduce our own specific continuing versions, unless we can in this way form and act out a sufficiently secure, stable story about our lives, we are like Darl, profoundly shaken in his sense of self. Similarly, unless we can coproduce such a narrative about death, we may be as anguished and grotesque as Vardaman. Without anyone to explain his mother's death consolingly to him, this child must improvise an story. He does so based on the coincidence of his experience in catching a fish on the day his mother dies. So he explains what is to him an unprecedented, grievous death in terms of something familiar to him: "My mother is a fish" (*AILD*, 74).

We can see here the reverse side to the power of stories and collective (shared) story conventions in shaping our lives. Vardaman's improvised explanation of his mother's death and yet somehow continuing life is uncanny. That is to say that this ministory of explanation is not a *coproduced* story, not a metaphor anyone around him shares. It is not based on a convention of his immediate society, in other words. (This point is emphasized by the fact that the informed reader can recognize traditional conventions of life-giving solidarity in the fish symbol, since Vardaman's family lacks these references, and in any case, it would be highly unconventional simply to say one's mother is a fish.)

Vardaman's absurd statement dramatizes how feeling is inadvertently, even comically, distorted when one lacks a convention available for sharing feelings with others. Within the rural community that Rachel Samson and Lula Armstid inhabit, no convention of speech is broken by their saying "It's *a* outrage" rather than "*an* outrage." For us as readers, however, the statement, violating our conventions of proper usage ("grammar"), produces a light static of humor that may "interfere with" the real sincerity of their intended message. But there is no narrative convention either inside the novel's world or in the reader's world to accommodate Vardaman's miniature explanatory tale readily. Consequently, our sense of his statement's sincerity of feeling coexists in contradiction with our sense of its absurdity.

We began discussion of convention with the idea, reinforced by Faulkner's own comment about this novel, that convention was simply a villain in our lives. Now, however, without at all denying the destructive potentials of convention, we have arrived at the other, positive side of the coin. Convention is the preestablished social channel of sharing necessary for sharing our feelings or thoughts and creating the basis for cooperative action, even if the aim of that action is to change specific conventions. Conventional formulations may distort and frustrate our feelings, thoughts, and actions, but so does the lack of such ready-made formulations, like words.

What's more, if we coproduce *ourselves* within our culture's shared stories, then the conventions that form the basis for sharing also form a basis for who we are. Conventions are not just "out there" in something merely external and public called "society." Conventions are "in here" as well, part of us, internal to our own private habits and shaping whatever they enable us not only to express but to feel and think. And society is "in here" with them. To see this is to expand and reinforce the points made earlier about Bundren secrecy as both desire and convention, and about the individual as a component of social being. Conventions are intrinsic to our feelings, lived with and lived out for so long that they seem entirely natural and not culturally derived. Feelings about death and treatment of the dead powerfully illustrate this fusion and confusion. Note that Rachel Samson's and Lula Armstid's quite genuine outrage at Anse—a feeling, amounting to physical disgust, that their self-esteem is affronted—arises as if naturally from an affront to their culture's conventions for treatment of the dead, which they have absorbed as part of their identity as members of the social body. Conventions for dealing with the dead are, in fact, quite specific to cultures and vary a great deal. Traditional cultural practices around the world range from abandonment and forgetting of the dead to ritualized putrefaction of the corpse, all these customs existing as elements of the different formative stories cultures tell about human existence.

Despite the fluid boundaries between people, and despite the fact that the conventions we absorb bind our lives radically with others' lives, the stories of the Bundrens' society tell of a dilemma. Everyone is shaped by and shapes others, everyone's voice echoes and is echoed by others; but caught between a cult of private self-sufficiency and a pull toward solidarity in collective action, every-one experiences alienation between and within self and other. To the degree that important feelings cannot be shared adequately or unthreateningly, the common efforts and achievements of people's lives are made hollow. But so enduring is the desire or need to make a more-than-illusory collective whole that, no matter how much balked in practice, it still finds an outlet in some way—though often as awkwardly and self-defeatingly as in Addie's image of people as "spiders dangling by their mouths from a beam, swinging and twisting and never touching" (*AILD*, 158).

Consequently, this novel tells of the clumsy provisional group efforts its people cobble together with sometimes heroic exertions. It suggests that, depending on the perspective one takes on this effort, one may be struck by the absurdity of its makeshifts and its excessive or clumsy energies, or one may be stirred by the motives, however grotesque in form, that may be discerned in all the fumbling. One may feel, in other words, that the action is grotesquely humorous or tragic, or both at once. The collective action may be as tragic or farcical, or both, as a country family's effort to take a wife and mother's decaying body on a long Mississippi July wagon journey through flood and fire to the cemetery. *As I Lay Dying*, telling this fundamentally simple action, makes it complex by offering all these perspectives, generated by the competing or collaborating stories that observers and participants tell and live out.

"I would be I," Addie says, meaning that she wishes not to be, as she sees Anse, merely "the shape and echo" of words. Our discussion has brought us to the point of saying that although Addie's desire not to be Anse is readily understandable, in an important sense she oversimplifies here. To be an "I" *is* to be the shape and echo of words, the words of others as well as our own, in the sense that we radically depend on others' stories and the conventions that make them possible. For good or ill, the "I" includes "he's" and "she's," "we's" and "they's."

Yet we can draw a correct implication from Addie's statement: in the framework of the dominant cult of private self-sufficiency, it can mean madness to be plunged into the contrary reality. For Darl the "I" that would be "I" finally becomes instead both "we" and "he" when Darl madly adopts his family's perspective to speak of himself as "our brother Darl" (*AILD*, 235–36). The novel also supports Addie's repugnance at unquestioned conventionality as a peril to the fluid life of the "I." Although convention is necessary, like a river channel, it also can all too easily divert the flow of desires and needs to which it gives form and power, blocking them and silting them over, just as a river channel may erode and impede its current. Perhaps one cultural master story above all performs this diversion, and we must now consider it.

# 7

# *Sacred Economics in Yoknapatawpha*

## PASSIONATE REVERSAL

Skeet MacGowan, rejecting Dewey Dell's offer of 10 dollars for an abortion, claims "I cant put no price on my knowledge and skill" (*AILD*, 229). He quibbles, of course, since although he takes no money he makes Dewey Dell trade her sexual favors for his bogus treatment. So extensive is the practice of trade, just about everything in Yoknapatawpha seems to be swappable. If the trade involves what seems at first glance to be "no price," no one should be deceived into thinking that a trade is not occurring, since symbolic goods and services and those with more immediately practical value circulate constantly. Consider Jewel's horse.

The meaning of symbolic wealth is exemplified in the emotional value that Jewel's horse has for him beyond its monetary or immediately practical worth—the same kind of emotional value a powerful, impressive car might have for Jewel's contemporaries in town. Conversely, to obtain the symbolic value of his horse, Jewel exchanges the utilitarian value of his services to Lon Quick. For Lon Quick, who was unable to give the untamable horse away until it attracted Jewel, the horse becomes an exchangeable surplus economic good—capital—like the eggs that Cora saves to make money to increase the net value of her flock. Capital—wealth capable of producing more wealth—in its symbolic form is illustrated in the intangible worth of someone's reputation, which may help him or her to obtain a tangible gain, as a person's reputation for honesty or cleverness may induce others to trust her or him with their money. Conversely, tangible wealth may be traded in the market place of repute to increase one's symbolic capital, one's "image," in the eyes of some.

Religion is an especially important storehouse of symbolic values in the world of this novel. Asked to comment on the similarity of the families of *As I Lay Dying* and *The Sound and the Fury*, Faulkner answered that the basis of the similarity was "the influence of a violent form of the Protestant religion, on politics . . . on the economy of the country" (Gwynn and Blotner, 121). In Faulkner's writings the mutual influences between religion, politics, and economics actually are more complex than this statement acknowledges. But a religious framework is indeed paramount in the mentality of his characters in *As I Lay Dying*. Symbolic and utilitarian goods are traded for each other on the basis of a fundamental story of sacred economics in the Bundren's culture. This cultural reality, we saw, begins to be established early in the novel in Cora's and Jewel's mental negotiations, as they attempt to participate in, and improve, God's giving and taking of lives and worldly and heavenly goods.

Anse, as he often does, provides the key. Here Anse encapsulates the master story, the wellspring of other stories, according to Anse as he contemplates the devastation of the violent rains:

> It's a hard country on man; it's hard. Eight miles of the sweat of his body washed up outen the Lord's earth, where the Lord Himself told him to put it. Nowhere in this sinful world can a honest, hard-working man profit. It takes them that runs the stores in the towns, doing no sweating, living off of them that sweats. It aint the hardworking man, the farmer. Sometimes I wonder why we keep at it. It's because there is a reward for us above, where they cant take their autos and such. Every man will be equal there and it will be taken from them that have and give to them that have not by the Lord.
>
> But it's a long wait, seems like. It's bad that a fellow must earn the reward of his right-doing by flouting hisself and his dead. . . . I am the chosen of the Lord, for who He loveth, so doeth He chastiseth. But I be durn if He dont take some curious ways to show it, seems like. (*AILD*, 97)

As in Cora's invocation of God's wrath on the town woman who doesn't keep her economic promise, the heart of this story is its plot of "passionate reversal." This plot amplifies one element of the Christian story and makes it into a framework for understanding social classes: in heaven, the last shall be first, and the first shall be last. (This is the usual phrase, but its source, Luke 13:30, is more qualified in the King James version: "There are last which shall be first, and there are first which shall be last.")

In the Yoknapatawpha countryfolk version of this reversal, there are three main geographical regions: country, town, and heaven. The country is the place of trial and hardship, where farmers work for the benefit of the powerful economic parasites in the town. Poor in utilitarian goods, the farmers earn symbolic capital in the form of spiritual solvency. Town is where earthly, more utilitarian goods are—autos, teeth, abortion pills, trains, bananas, graphophones, and even spouses. Town is simultaneously an earthly counterpart of heaven's promised reward and a perversion of it, since the town's promised rewards represent the farmers' sweat stolen from them. Heaven is the place where the dominance of town over country is reversed, where social justice will finally prevail as the stolen sweat is recovered from the townspeople and for the countrypeople is transformed into symbolic wealth as their reward in heaven. The sweat stolen from the farmers in the town, or washed away from the land by a heaven-sent flood, is an ultimate capital to be exchanged into gain, saved as a profit in heaven. (The wry humor here of course is that Anse, our prime authority in the novel for this story, at this point in his life makes sure that he never sweats.)

The formulaic greeting of the mourners arriving for Addie's funeral leaves out "and the Lord taketh away" from the Biblical citation, stressing instead what the event of death means in spiritual terms: "The Lord giveth" (*AILD*, 76) in heaven what he has taken away from poor countrypeople like Addie during their lives.

The implicit economics and politics of this master story make God into a distant feudal monarch who will eventually, in his own time, right the wrongs of the local barons, the small-town rich people—the owners of the cotton gins, banks, and main stores—who had come into their own in the twenties.[9]

By this time politicoeconomic power had shifted considerably away from the previously dominant large landowners to the small-town rich, with whom they often made common cause, and both were themselves often at the mercy of distant Northern industries that had long since extensively colonized the South economically if not politically. Further, neither the Tulls nor the Bundrens are tenant farmers, but own their own land. Yet the countryfolk represented by Cora and Anse still think in terms of a stern but ultimately benevolent "Old Marster" (*AILD*, 34). This is a divine landowner who will punish the wicked barons and reward the faithful laborers on his lands, who grow "God's own victuals" (*AILD*, 33) despite flood, drought, insects, and market manipulations by greedy human parasites, all sent by Old Master to test the laborers' power, in Anse's words, to "keep at it" as laborers. Their endurance is a promissory note they can redeem for a heavenly reward, on one hard condition. As Anse says, they must "flout" themselves—flout themselves by swallowing their sense of outrage and grievance against their economic oppression, as MacGowan tells Dewey Dell to swallow her turpentine as a "treatment" (*AILD*, 230).

Vardaman's childish jumble of half-understood class discontent has been absorbed from the conflation of religious and immediately practical economics he hears around him. His thoughts on his family's poverty are instructive both for what they include and for what they leave out:

> Dewey Dell said we will get some bananas. The train is behind the glass, red on the track. . . . Pa said flour and sugar and coffee costs so much. Because I am a country boy because boys in town. Bicycles. Why do flour and sugar and coffee cost so much when he is a country boy. "Wouldn't you ruther have some bananas, instead?" Bananas are gone, eaten. Gone. . . . "Why aint I a town boy, pa?" I said. God made me. I did not said to God to made me in the country. If He can make the train, why cant He make them all in the town because flour and sugar and coffee. "Wouldn't you ruther have bananas?" . . . [My mother] went away. "Did she go as far as town?" "She went further than town." "Did all those rabbits and possums go further than town?" God made the rabbits and possums. He made the train. Why must he make a different place for them to go if she is just like the rabbit. (*AILD*, 59–60)

What Vardaman is trying to get straight are the rules of equivalence and exchange. In simpler language, what is equal to what? What can be substituted or swapped for what? But he cannot be confident that there are any such exchangeable items. To use a doubly weighted word in the novel, nothing *balances* in Vardaman's accounting. Although bananas at this time were a luxury fruit for poor Mississippi farming people, to Vardaman bananas cannot substitute for the beauty, the symbolic value, of a toy train. Flour and sugar and coffee are cash items that cash-poor farmers could not produce themselves and often went into debt to buy. His family's utilitarian need for them outweighs his desire for the train, although town boys even have bicycles. Similarly, is his mother equivalent, or is she not, to the dead rabbits and possums he has seen, and what can right the balance of her loss? God could right all these balances somehow, he senses, and he is astounded that God has neglected to put him and everyone else in town, where obviously things balance out better.

If we compare Vardaman's thoughts with Anse's account of sacred economics, it's clear that what's missing from Vardaman's fragmentary story and its geography is, first, heaven, the place of economic reversal after death, a place Vardaman can only fumble at as something "further than town." Closely related is that he has no clear cultural concept of human death, which as an event is nevertheless so prominent in his story and so prominently missing from Anse's and Cora's. Vardaman's naive failure to understand the cultural conventions of exchange makes the rudiments of symbolic and utilitarian exchanges stand out all the more clearly. He has yet to learn that in his culture's stories, death is decisive. Death is the sharply drawn dividing line that allows injustice to be turned into justice. Death is the boundary line beyond which the rich cannot "take their autos and such," and all the symbolic and utilitarian exchanges are finally made to balance out once and for all by divine power alone.

This crucial role of death in the cultural Old Master story is questioned by the view of death and life as interlinked social processes. This view, which Peabody first states and the novel as a whole ratifies, blurs the line of death just as it blurs lines between genres and conventions and the cultural assumptions embedded in them. Once this crux is put in question, so is the whole rationale for a fated endurance of social oppression—bearing it as an inevitable burden, flouting oneself and one's dead, on the grounds that this is a religious duty in conformity with God's plan.

Submission to this supposedly divinely ordained rationale and plan comes hard, however, as is evident in the complaints and questions of Cora, Anse, and Vardaman. Vernon Tull, too, mentally protests when Cora accounts for Vardaman's aberrant behavior after Addie's death by claiming it is God's "judgment" punishing Anse through his child (*AILD*, 64). Tull thinks: "If it's a judgment, it aint right. Because the Lord's got more to do than that. He's bound to have. Because the only burden Anse Bundren's ever had is himself. And when folks talks him low, I think to myself he aint that less of a man or he couldn't a bore himself this long. It aint right. I be durn if it is. Because He said Suffer little children to come unto Me dont make it right, neither" (*AILD*, 66).

Even while Tull protests that punishing children for their parent's misdeeds is unjust, the pattern of his thought is plainly derived from the assumption that burdens and suffering are prerequisites for coming to the Lord. More important, the ability to bear them has the highest value, even, ironically, redeeming Anse. That Anse is to be respected for having the fortitude to bear himself is a humorous secular version of the master plot of reversal in which the power to bear oppression turns earthly lowliness into heavenly stature. Significantly, Tull interprets Jesus' statement that children should be suffered to come—literally meaning, in the English of the King James Bible, *allowed* to come—to mean that they must suffer before they can approach God. What is being protested by Tull, clearly, is the apparent injustice of God's management of a particular case of burdening people, not the basic reversal plot itself in which burdens and sweat are ultimate symbolic capital.

Also significant is Tull's further association of ideas as he moves from his own protest to his recognition, as noted before, that Cora would like to take over and improve God's management. He ends this way: "And I reckon she would make a few changes, no matter how He was running it. And I reckon they would be for man's good. Leastways, we would have to like them. Leastways, we might as well go on and make like we did" (*AILD*, 66). Might makes right, in other words, and we must flout ourselves by pretending to like this inevitable state of affairs, whether the Old Master is God or someone playing God. Tull's line of thought is dangerous to his peace of mind, as he knows, and in effect he is warning himself when he declares that Darl's trouble is that he thinks too much. Tull tells himself, in words that may remind us of Addie's preference for action, that "the Lord aimed for [people] to do and not to spend too much time thinking" (*AILD*, 64).

The farmers gathered for Addie's funeral think the same way, as they, like Anse, foresee the waste of their labor by the hard rains and flooding. Yet the problem their anonymous voices begin to address and then skirt is precisely the curbs placed on their doing, their action:

> *Washed clean outen the ground [the crop] will be. Seems like something is always happening to it.*
>
> *Course it does. That's why it's worth anything. If nothing didn't happen and everybody made a big crop, do you reckon it would be worth the raising?*
>
> *Well, I be durn if I like to see my work washed outen the ground, work I sweat over.*
>
> *It's a fact. A fellow wouldn't mind seeing it washed up if he could just turn on the rain himself.*
>
> *Who is that man can do that? Where is the color of his eyes?*
>
> *Ay. The Lord made it to grow. It's Hisn to wash up if He sees it fitten so. (AILD, 80)*

Compare this collective spin-off from the master story with the individual spin-offs—Cora's, Anse's, and Tull's, as well as Vardaman's photographic negative of the story. The habit of thought, consistently, is one of dramatic reversal in which resentments are followed by consolations. The farmer's thought pattern runs, again in a familiar sequence, from immediately practical economics to the symbolic economics of religion. One speaker says that repeated disaster strikes the farmers, but another replies that the scarcity produced by natural disasters increases the crop's value. A complaint then follows that it's still frustrating to see your efforts and powers so wasted. At this point, without missing a beat, the dialogue jumps immediately to the level of supernatural power: if destruction and waste are inevitable, the next speaker says in effect, it would be better to have the power to impose them on yourself, "to turn on the rain [yourself]."

In this half-playing, half-wishful banter descended from old Southwest frontier exaggeration, we have reached once more the point of self-flouting, here taken to the degree of self-destructiveness, a paradoxical kind of godlike power over one's own fate. At this juncture, in fact, we are not far from Darl's fatalistic desire for calamity and Addie's masochism, or Anse's ability to take a sort of satisfaction in the potential frustration the flooded river presents: "I be durn if he didn't act like he was proud of it, *like he had made the river rise himself*" (*AILD*, 100, italics added; cf. 69, 109). Once more, the Bundrens are "crazy" or eccentric not because they are radically different from their neighbors but because they are, so to speak, so excessively identical to them, larger-than-Yoknapatawpha embodiments of life in rural Yoknapatawpha.

The farmers' conversation reaches a turning point when it expresses a desire to be powerful enough to flout yourself by taking over the role of the Old Master who turns on the rains. This bantering-but-serious flirtation with rebelliousness is then called to order in words that paraphrase God's warnings to Job in the Bible. Everyone is reminded that no human being can do this, and the crops are the supreme landowner's to grow and destroy at pleasure.

This conversation beautifully illustrates the meaning of a red herring, for it turns on a false lead luring the farmers away from the trail they are following. Here the red herring is symbolic, specifically religious, value. The warning of God's unquestionable power shows that symbolic values, however valid they may be in themselves, have been inappropriately introduced here to divert the conversation from the pressing practical matter at hand: the excessive, wasted labor the farmers endure in order to support their families. The specific economics relating weather, scarcity, and prices for one's goods and labor have been in a few words swapped first for magical wishes for the power to act supernaturally and then for the religious economics of God's ownership and unchallengeable power.

Practical matters cannot even be thought about because the speakers have made this equivalent to rebelling against God. This too-rapid swapping of immediately practical issues for ultimate symbolic ones not only censors further thought about the concrete realities of their situation but eliminates any action besides a dogged continuance in conventional ways.

Such built-in self-censoring in their thought forbids them to examine their customs and other conventions and so condemns them to the inert conventionality that, while it comforts them with familiarity, flouts and wears away all their other desires and needs.

The remarkable group substitution of symbolic for utilitarian economics erases the very level, the marketplace, at which the farmers together could have planned and taken cooperative practical action to try to sell their sweat for better prices. This level does appear in the master story according to Anse in the guise of "them that runs the stores in the towns, doing no sweating, living off them that sweats." But although Anse designates the marketplace, it does little good. He also quickly exchanges it wholesale for the symbolic values of ultimate justice, where stolen and wasted sweat is reenvisioned as a surplus with long-term capital value. The story of the sacred economics substitutes for and cancels out practical political and economic action.

The farmers' running-together of economics and religion, then, distracts them from the very possibility of attempting any collective action—any action, that is, beyond a stubborn bearing of sacred but self-flouting burdens. The outsized mirror of this persistence is the Bundrens' indescribable mixture of heroism and absurdity in carrying out their sacred, self-flouting journey.

Comparing all these individual and group accounts calls attention to the neglected actual marketplace beginning in the town and extending, as Vardaman would say, "further than town." This marketplace extends, however, not into heaven but into the arena of politics and its embedded economic conventions. This is the arena to which the political connotations of Vardaman's name also call our attention.

Of the many stories linked to young Vardaman Bundren's extraordinary namesake, the Mississippi politician and newspaperman James K. Vardaman, one above all forms a subtext of Faulkner's novel: the one called "the rise of the rednecks" or "the revolt of the rednecks." Vardaman's name points us to a parallel between Faulkner's text and this cultural story as well to a marked exclusion of part of the story by Faulkner's text. The parallel is the pattern we have just uncovered, in which people are distracted from effective political and economic action by symbolic values that both draw them together in a comforting view and disable them at the same time.

Vardaman was a hero to people like the Bundrens and their neighbors, a major leader of the Southern political uprising of poor white people. Not only did these small farmers and blue-collar workers name children after him and call him "the White Chief," but long after he had served as governor (1904–1908) and U. S. senator (1912–18), his brand of politics was called "Vardamanism" in Mississippi. As Faulkner wrote *As I Lay Dying*, an invalid Vardaman had lain dying for three years (he was to die shortly before the novel's publication). A corrupt practitioner of Vardamanism, Theodore Bilbo, was governor, having succeeded the man who had earlier defeated him, Henry L. Whitfield, who died in office and to whom we will return shortly.

For Vardaman's time and place, in many ways he had remarkably progressive politics, working to alleviate economic and social oppression by supporting education, women's suffrage, child-labor legislation (it's fitting in this respect that the poor child in this novel is named after him), regulation of corporations, fairer interest rates, better rural roads, and state funded mental health care. More than these particular programs, he gave (white) small farmers and other working people a real sense of hope by showing them their power to band together as a formidable political force. But combined with this progressivism, which appealed to their ability to recognize their best economic interests and organize themselves in collective political action, was the White Chief's demagoguery, especially a virulent racism, which appealed to their capacity for self-delusion. This racism, unfortunately, was a large part of what bonded Vardaman and his followers together as a collective force.[10]

In Faulkner's novel, as discussed earlier, the effect of the white religious master story is to censor the political and economic thinking of the Yoknapatawpha farmers. By exclusively promising satisfaction of their class grievances in the afterlife, this story distracts them from taking more immediate effective measures together. Vardamanism counteracts this story with a position akin to "God helps those that help themselves." In Vardaman's activist view, belief in heavenly justice does not substitute for but rather complements efforts to gain social justice here and now.

Nevertheless, Vardaman's name reminds us of the corresponding distraction, racism, which intertwined with religion, economics, and politics. According to the master reversal plot in which the last shall be first, one would expect that blacks, because they were even more socially oppressed than the burdened white small farmers, would have earned the highest symbolic value, prestige, in their eyes. But the reversal plot is blind to the logic of this conclusion. There is a racist escape clause to the effect that the last shall be first, except that, supposedly, the Bible mandates white supremacy politically and economically.

The master story thus delivers a one-two punch to potentially effective anger at economic oppression. One part of the story delays the satisfaction of anger until ultimate justice after death. The other directs it away from its real focus, economic and political issues including the burdens of class, to a pseudofocus on blacks as competitors who must be kept down.

In a story written before *As I Lay Dying*, Faulkner's narrator explicitly describes the poor whites' racism as "an antipathy . . . at once biblical, political, and economic: the three compulsions—the harsh unflagging land broken into sparse intervals by spells of demagoguery and religio-neurotic hysteria—which shaped and coerced their gaunt lives. A mystical justification of the need to feel superior to someone somewhere, you see."[11] In this master story of a master race, white supremacism has falsely identified the problems actually facing whites and, while furnishing them with a kind of mystical collectivist comfort in the mirage of group superiority, has made them vulnerable to a demagoguery that only multiplies their problems.

Faulkner subjects this red herring of racism to a potent analysis in the next novel he writes, *Light in August* (1932), where racism and what he called "a violent form of the Protestant religion" combine with horrific results. Later, he can present white Southern Protestantism, significantly detached from race issues, in a more genial light, as in the commercially appealing story "Shingles for the Lord" (1942). In *As I Lay Dying*, perhaps because of the economic deadline under which he worked in 1929–30 and because he was himself still digesting the implications of what he had already written and was in the process of writing, Faulkner concentrates on religion and economics, two of the three shaping and coercing compulsions of the master story in which racism is embedded. But he supplies place markers and signposts, like Vardaman's name, that send both writer and the reader on to the rest of the larger story involving politics and racism.

Another such indicator occurs shortly after the Bundrens' stinking wagon has passed the signs promising the commodity rewards to be found in Jefferson—"the drug stores, the clothing stores, the patent medicine and the garages and cafes" (*AILD*, 209).[12] On the margins of the town it begins to pass the homes of black people, who emerge with outraged faces and voices. "Jewel has been looking from side to side," Darl reports, "now his head turns forward and I can see his ears taking on a still deeper tone of furious red" (*AILD*, 212). The wagon passes three black men in the road, and it is at this point that one of them asks indignantly "Great God . . . what they got in that wagon?" Something curious happens. Jewel doesn't attack the black man who not only has spoken these words but has provided him with a target to stand for all the blacks' humiliating reactions that have been reddening Jewel's ears. Instead, he vents his anger against a white man, whom he at first inadvertently insults but then purposely flouts by accusing him of snobbery: "Thinks because he's a goddamn town fellow. . . . Son of a bitch" (*AILD*, 213). Jewel could have easily explained that his first insult, "Son of a bitches," wasn't directed at the white man and then gone on to confront the black man, and white solidarity against blacks might have given his explanation credibility. Instead, Jewel eagerly substitutes town fellow for black man as the focus of anger. In a society that operates such a large chain of substitutions, this surprising exchange bears examination.

It might be supposed, of course, that Jewel simply is not a racist. But this misses the point, since Jewel wants to avenge a perceived insult, beyond any question of its source. It seems that Faulkner is accomplishing several aims here. First, he is highlighting the strength of class antagonism between country and town dwellers for generations of insults by playing off the reader's expectation that Southern white antagonism toward blacks will, or must, automatically outweigh all else. Class resentment and strife have been on the collective Bundren mind throughout the journey, gathering momentum for their entrance into this substitute heaven of sweat converted into commodities. And Dewey Dell has just changed into her Sunday clothes, in a defensive attempt to "pass" for a townsperson.

Second, as with the use of Vardaman's name, the novel is drawing attention to the link between the two antagonisms as well as to the diversions of collective action. This happens, fittingly, at the very point where country meets town. A white farmer turning away from a black man to confront white class snobbery—this act might have provided an image of a more constructive reversal, turning from the empty symbolism of anger at blacks to practical anger at an unjust system operating through the townspeople and oppressing blacks even more. Instead, Jewel acts as an individual against an individual, and his family's solidarity with him is applied solely to prevent a pointless distraction from their goal, as Darl defuses the situation.

Third, when Darl says of Jewel's apparent confusion in challenging the white man, "It is as though Jewel had gone blind for the moment," the novel directs us to the invisibility of blacks, or their presence on the margins, in white society. In line with its general methods, the novel here stages a disruption in the reader's conventional expectations to make visible, if only momentarily, an invisible "normal" state of affairs. This scene uncovers one of white society's main family secrets, a place not supposed to exist in the geography of sacred economics. The scene discloses blacks existing on the margins between town and country, being neither "town folk"—that is, the white privileged class—nor country folk—that is, rural whites whose outrage will be recognized and vindicated after death. The black community is itself outraged by these country folks' behavior, but its outrage quickly drops from their sight, into the mental crevices where family secrets are kept and more blindness breeds.

In this section and the novel as a whole, if Faulkner doesn't give us anything like a full-fledged treatment of racism as part of sacred economics and its shackling conventionality, he does the next best thing. He signals that the marginal existence of blacks in this novel represents the disclosure of a family secret in the cultural story of stories. And he uses the occasion to underscore the frustration of the desire or need for collective action.

Making black people socially invisible—except on occasions, like elections, when they could be inveighed against as the enemy—was one means for poor whites to blinker their under-standing that their own precarious economic situation was all too similar to that of blacks. One historian notes that after the Civil War and Reconstruction (i.e., by about 1876), in the South

> most blacks found themselves tied to the land as sharecroppers. They soon found that they had traded slavery for serfdom. Share-croppers were as much at the mercy of white landowners as slaves had been to their masters. . . . From the outset, [these blacks] were *beholden to the landlord* for a "furnish," credit extended until the crop was harvested. The landlord . . . kept the books and sold the cotton against which the furnish was tallied. Almost always, the cropper[s] found [themselves] *ever deeper in debt to the landlord*. If the system was not exactly slavery, it certainly promoted economic bondage. (Skates, 121; italics added)

The historian goes on to say, in agreement with several others, that the revolt of the rural white people beginning at the turn of the century was directed against the parallel system of economic beholdenness and bondage enveloping all small farmers, black or white. "A credit system that required the farmer to pledge his crop to the merchant to receive credit to produce the crop ground down the small farmer into the ranks of the sharecroppers. Sharecrop-ping developed after the Civil War as a system of black labor. By 1930 half of Mississippi's sharecroppers were white. By 1900 a conservative political machine dominated state politics, favored the planter over the small farmer, and curried favor with the railroads, banks, and merchants by enacting favorable legislation and tax policies" (Skates, 121).

The Bundrens and their neighbors are not described as share-croppers. But the terrible economic conditions produced by their political and economic circumstances, combined with disasters like the actual great floods of the late twenties, make farmers like them vulnerable to debt and the seizing of their possessions for nonpay-ment. The horrible possibility is always before them that they will then fall into the serfdom that blacks epitomize to them. Black people are the frightening reminders of the bizarre and terrible fate of being technically free and yet in bondage. White racism feeds on itself in a vicious circle as the white mental association of blacks with the whites' own potential degrading bondage breeds a self-fulfilling "us versus them" mentality.

So "As long as [blacks] represented even a possible threat . . . white conservatives and radical small farmers were forced into an alliance of race—a coalition that defied economic self-interest. . . . By attempting to uplift the poor whites without altering the status of Mississippi blacks . . . [Vardaman and Bilbo] assured the failure of their programs. No more than white Mississippians of a later generation did the followers of Vardaman and Bilbo recognize the unbreakable link between black oppression and white poverty" (Skates, 126–27).

Little wonder, then, that racism involves keeping blacks out of the whites' mind if not literally out of sight. No wonder, either, that as psychological compensation for their fragile economic independence, white farmers could easily exaggerate their self-reliance into touchy pride. Little wonder, further, the compensatory anachronistic idea of God as an ultimately fair Old Master landlord for whom they sharecrop spiritually and who extends even Anse an open line of credit. No wonder, finally, that the fear of being beholden in general could take root in the economic fear that monetary debt would literally turn them into sharecroppers, beholden to the point of neoslavery. Understanding these foundations of the Bundren social microcosm does not make the family any less bizarre in their immediate impact, but it does perhaps reveal them as even more tragically terrible. It is, above all, a whole side of society that is unmasked as bizarre and terrible.

What Faulkner only hints at besides racism—but what must be hinted at because it was historically inseparable—is the positive element of Vardaman's politics: the progressive, positive solidarity in action among the lower economic classes that this politics accomplished. Vardaman's name is one of the novel's signs that testify to the importance of collective action as well as the inadequacy of its imitations in Yoknapatawpha. In keeping with the novel's general indirect methods, the name *Vardaman* draws our attention to this lack and, to borrow Addie's words in a more favorable sense, it points us generally to the absent shape of action that would fill this lack. The novel works too indirectly and undidactically, of course, to indicate that this shape specifically fits the positive dimension of Vardaman's politics. But these positive politics

97

based on economic change are a general analogy for the sort of fruitful collective action lacking—worn away, censored, and diverted—in the world of the Bundrens.

The name *Whitfield* is another such signpost, this one pointing especially to the social burdens borne by women and to the process of their emancipation. As state superintendent of education around the turn of the century, Henry L. Whitfield sought to improve the hard conditions of farmers, with an emphasis on the condition of farm women, through practical education. Among his several measures to improve the lot of teachers, such as Addie and Cora had been, was advocacy of "normal school" education for teach-ers—over half of which, it's perhaps worth noting, was financed by the Peabody fund.

Whitfield's dedication to education for women was demon-strated further in his years as the president of the state women's college. His long service in this position ended in 1920 when he was forced out by the new governor, Lee Russell, for having refused to pressure the college faculty to support Russell's election. (Russell, as noted before, was originally from the hill farming area where Faulkner locates the Bundrens, he had begun his political career in the law firm of Faulkner's grandfather, and like Vardaman he was supported by the influential Falkner family.)

Whitfield's subsequent victory over Bilbo in the 1923 gover-nor's race was aided by an endorsement by the invalided James Vardaman. Vardaman favored Whitfield over Vardaman's former ally even though Whitfield, while being a standard-issue segrega-tionist, opposed the vicious racism of Vardaman and his imitators. Even more important in Whitfield's election, according to a widely held view, was the powerful organized support of newly enfran-chised women.

Like the famous eighteenth-century preacher and founder of Methodism, George Whitefield, Henry Whitfield was renowned for his religious fervor. As college president he frequently took the pulpit on campus. As governor he preached at evangelical camp meetings like the one at which Cora tells us Addie's Whitfield strove mightily with her. Further, among the reforms Henry Whitfield instituted were improved facilities for the treatment of the mentally ill and handicapped. His last public speech was at the ground-breaking ceremony for a new state hospital, whose construction entailed the eventual moving of the asylum from Jackson. When Whitfield died, his reputation for activism in both religion and politics led him to be eulogized as one who stood for deeds over mere words.[13] Here again are shades of Addie Bundren and her milieu—up to a significant point.

The combined political and religious connotations of the name of Addie's lover reinforce the connection between Addie's unusual sexual mysticism and the seemingly more normal yet mystified economics of her milieu. No doubt both the real and the fictional Whitfields would have been outraged at Addie's version of participating in a sacred action that includes all actions whatsoever—collective indeed. But like the Vardaman reference, the Whitfield connection offers parallels and contrasts to display what is missing in action from Addie's milieu as from her scheme.

On the one hand, there is the women's cooperation that rallied around the historical Whitfield and helped empower and effectively channel independent outlooks like Addie's. On the other hand, there is her vengeful and private scheme in which, through sexual relations with her Whitfield, she mentally and emotionally participates in the doing that goes terribly along the earth. Taken together, the Vardaman and Whitfield allusions underscore the pull toward collective action widespread in the Bundrens' society. Simultaneously, the allusions spotlight the pervasive habit of symbolic forms of thought that, like the burial journey, poorly substitute for the desired and needed sharing of meaningful action with others.

Faulkner's critique of the cultural story accords with much of the account that historians and others give about the differences between Northern and Southern religion. Northern evangelical and other religion has been more inclined to be involved in social action and reform. Southern evangelical Protestantism has tended to put more emphasis on the instant of the individual's emotional conversion experience of union with Jesus. Camp meetings such as those that Addie attends typically use the reinforcement of shared emotionalism inspired by highly symbol-charged preaching to lead the individual to the climactic conversion experience. It has become a commonplace to observe that often through the entire process there runs a sometimes barely concealed undercurrent of sexuality.

For all of Addie's eccentricity at one level, her poetic account of individual ecstatic union with Whitfield and the collectivist divine life force is a page out of the master cultural text. Here collectivism is symbolic, emotional oneness. Black evangelical churches, in moving beyond this point, present the important exception. With the assistance of more typically Northern habits of activism, the Southern civil rights movement drew upon the communal feeling of the churches to forge a symbol-centered solidarity leading to effective collective action against racism.

As this last instance reminds us, nothing in our discussion depends on a simple contrast between symbolic thinking or behavior and something else that is not symbolic. This would be to duplicate Addie's false split between words and action. To write and to speak words is to act, to act through symbols. Actions too resonate with symbolic meaning, as Addie's own deeds illustrate. Like all politics, and indeed all human endeavors, the positive politics of the white farmers' and women's movements are replete with symbolic actions and images. The real contrast is between those habits of symbolic thinking and acting that are also more practically effective, more likely actually to redress injustices, and those symbolic habits that, for a variety of reasons, mystify problems and serve only as psychological stopgaps. The difference is between red herrings and real leads.

In reality, of course, one is often hard to tell from the other, and there are times when, at least temporarily, only such stopgaps are available to allow people to endure their situation. Accordingly, the novel gives Addie's kind of anguished imagining a powerful voice. This imaginative sympathy with her potent imagination, however, is accompanied by the simultaneous critique of its tragic limitations. For the novel to do otherwise would be to falsify her real desires and needs and in so doing flout itself.

## CASHING IN

Addie has rejected conventional belief in an afterlife of rewards and punishments, but in word, thought, and deed she still continues the deep patterns of the cultural master story. Further, what happens to her body and the family's various relationships to it play off these patterns.

She loves her firstborn, Cash, in a way that his name suggests: like his name and his craft, carpentry, he provides immediate practical benefits and emotional satisfaction for Addie. In a way that Addie approves, he is verbally undemonstrative, preferring to show his feeling for her not in words but in deeds—getting the manure for her to grow flowers and building the coffin before her eyes. He has, so to speak, cash value. On (most) immediately practical matters, he is reliable, and as noted before he can be insightful about people. The major revealing exception is his own complicity in the mistreatment of his broken leg, where the social symbolic value of displaying tough self-reliance both as an individual and as part of his family's efforts overrides his practicality.

Cash's predominant blind spot, however, is symbolic matters that interfere with immediate practicality or lack an immediate practicality that he can see. The pan of manure fertilizer and the coffin are of course symbols of his love for Addie, but, typically, they are also immediately utilitarian. For Cash, practicality is in itself a symbolic value. What Cash cannot understand is well represented when the women reverse Addie's body in the coffin and so cancel out the balance he has crafted into her "box" with loving practicality. They do so for their own symbolic reasons, so Addie can be buried in her best clothes, her wedding gown. For readers who also see here a reference to preparing to meet the Biblical bridegroom, Jesus (Matthew 25:1–13), this reversal of her body may point to the other reversal in the cultural master narrative. Not for the last time in the novel, a symbolic anticipation of the afterlife gets in the way of more immediately practical measures, and partly as a result Addie's body does fall out of the wagon into the river. Mild-mannered Cash is, in his own way, outraged long before this spill actually occurs: "Them durn women," he fumes at the funeral (*AILD*, 80).

The separate cultural spheres of men and women are shown in the gender segregations in the funeral service and in the fact that Cash and the women preparing Addie's body could not cooperate to arrive at some arrangement that would express their values as well as his. Notice that apparently Cash fails even to try to tell them of the problem, much less to get their cooperation, and so do the other men to whom he complains.

Cash is reliably practical later when he says that it would have been better for Addie's body to have been lost in the river or the fire and implicitly faults Jewel for saving her both times. But Cash arrives at this conclusion, however correct it may be, without showing any understanding of what Addie's body and its preservation mean to Jewel. This kind of symbolic value is beyond Cash's horizon. Again, and more important, Cash has good practical reason on his side when he deplores Darl's burning of the Gillespies' barn, though Cash can understand that it would have been best to rid the family of her body before they become subject to further humiliation by scandalizing Jefferson. Considering how precarious the farmers' economic circumstances are, this barn-burning could well make the difference for the Gillespies between continuing as small landowners and falling into economic serfdom. So too, Darl's barn-burning has potentially put his own family in grave economic danger. The novel gives us no reason to treat such immediately practical considerations lightly.

But neither are we encouraged to be blind to, or take lightly, the symbolic values that led Darl to his desperate act. He expresses these in telling Vardaman that Addie in the coffin is praying to God to let her lay down her life. That is, after the public humiliation that her body has received, Darl feels that the Addie he remembers, who still lives in his mind, would have wanted to be hidden "from the sight of man" (*AILD*, 197). Her shameful continuation as an object in the family's and public's eyes has become a danger to her life in their memory, a burden to be laid down.

Nor are we encouraged to see Darl's severe punishment as merely a comeuppance for doing a poor and wasteful job of burning, which thus failed to produce the desired results. Cash, however, does this in his craft-based judgment: "It was bad. A fellow cant get away from a shoddy job. He cant do it. I tried to tell [Darl]." Cash's condemnation of a shoddy job, like his outrage at the women's supposed impracticality, is apparently the bottom line for him. But for all its practicality, there is a cultural symbolic line beneath it, as we see when Cash continues in revealing imagery: "Because there aint nothing justifies the deliberate destruction of what a man has built with his own sweat and stored the fruit of his sweat into" (*AILD*, 221). Cash is far from being conspicuously religious, but his secular religion and morality of taking pride in one's craft draw strongly from the cultural story here. The images of wasted sweat versus sweat stored away like fruit, as symbolic capital, are straight out of the story of stories.

The story of stories can be told and lived in many versions, however, and some of them are so incommunicable to others that they are judged insane. Practical-minded Cash is limited by his ethics of "good job versus bad job" to the point of blindness about symbolic values like those of Jewel and Darl. But Cash goes on to say that he isn't sure that anyone has the right to judge what's insane and what isn't: "It's like there was a fellow in every man that's done a-past the sanity and the insanity, that watches the sane and the insane doings of that man with the same horror and the same astonishment."

If everyone in this novel is a limited, privatized fragment of the collective social being, that shared superidentity may be hinted at here in Cash's image of "a fellow" in everyone transcending each person's sanity or insanity. In this scene those limits and their accompanying blind spots are revealed first in Darl when he is astonished into laughter at the absurdity of Cash's narrow practicality and lack of understanding, and second when Cash grumbles, "I be durn if I could see anything to laugh at" (*AILD*, 221). Cash's "sanity" in this scene invites from us "the same horror and the same astonishment" that Darl's "insanity" does. Cash cannot understand that laughter may spring from horror and astonishment, and he lacks awareness of what his own limits are, but he is rare in understanding that his limits, like everyone's, may be as bizarre and terrible as the different ways Jewel and Darl treat Addie's body.

Cash has the strengths and limitations of cash value, both for Addie and for us. Jewel, however, is even more favored by Addie than Cash is. Jewel's name also suggests value, but not simply immediate cash value. For Addie he has a symbolic worth rather like the beauty of a jewel that is also a storehouse of future worth: a jewel can be enjoyed symbolically and also ultimately cashed in. Jewel's horse helps to reveal this meaning in the career of exchanges he undergoes. He is first earned by Jewel's sweat and then enjoyed by Jewel for his symbolic value as an image of what

Jewel wants to be—powerfully active and untamable, with over-tones of potent sexuality. Finally, the horse is cashed in by Anse when the family needs mules to get to town and its rewards. So too, Jewel is to Addie the living embodiment of her symbolic action of sexual relations with Whitfield, with both the act and the son connecting her to her God's "love and His beauty and His sin." Further, in her earthly religion, as she tells Cora, if Jewel's wild-ness and gestures of independence make him her "cross," her suffering, this will be redeemed ultimately when he is her "salvation": "He will save me from the water and from the fire. Even though I have laid down my life, he will save me" (*AILD*, 154).

Addie's language here seems simply clairvoyant, since Jewel literally performs these rescues of her corpse, but her images of water and fire are traditional symbols for salvation (cf. Isaiah 43:1 and Psalms 66:12). As the novel does, Addie uses conventional reli-gious images and ideas unconventionally. Here the usage leaves a large margin for interpretation. Perhaps, despite the conventionality of the water and fire images for salvation, Addie's remark is among several moments of clairvoyance in time, one of the novel's own unconventional conventions. Or perhaps Addie means that although Jewel is her cross in life, as she nears death the thought of him and all he symbolizes to her will redeem her life to herself. Or perhaps both of these interpretations are correct, one focusing on her physical being, death, and salvation from disaster and the other on her social being, death, and salvation from a convention-burdened life. At any rate, the immediate point is that Jewel has ultimate practical value for Addie.

Here, however, there is no reason to cash in the jewel in order to get its practical value. That is, Jewel's symbolic value is psycho-logically the same as his practical value for Addie because both values are interchangeable in her mind. He has practical value for her as a psychological comfort, and he has this value because of his private meaning for her, his symbolic value. When it is purely in the mind, as in heaven, the symbolic simply is the practical value—there is no other. Jewel does not have to be cashed in or traded for a practical benefit. His symbolic meaning is that practi-cal benefit.

What happens in Addie's mind also happens on her body's journey, but it is inverted. Jewel has primarily practical value for the family as a whole in doing his share and more to get Addie to her destination. Here, too, he does not have to be cashed in or traded for something else. Instead, two substitutes are cashed in for him. One is his symbolic alter ego, the horse. The other is Darl, the living person who acts imaginatively through Jewel and for whom Jewel has the great symbolic value of love-hate. Darl is like unwanted surplus value that gets exchanged for the family's freedom from economic ruin, their possible liability for the Gillespie barn. The swapping of children that Addie began with the birth of Jewel extends far beyond her death.

Addie's body is the centerpiece in this round of trades. As the conventional object of reverence, her body is the family's primary symbolic capital, a surplus tradable for both practical advantage and added symbolic capital. Anse will illustrate.

Anse opines that "nowhere in this sinful world can a honest, hard-working man profit," but he certainly seeks gains from Addie's body. As readers too rarely see, he is after more than teeth and a new wife. Like Addie, he wants to combine symbolic and practical rewards, and the journey combines both for him as Jewel does for her. Following Addie's death Anse simply could have stolen Cash's phonograph money and/or Dewey Dell's abortion money, as he eventually does, and immediately gone to town on his own to get teeth and a wife complete with phonograph, as he eventually does. What Anse wants inseparably from these gains is that rare commodity in his life, prestige. This is what is promised in his role as chief mourner and bearer of Addie's body to the grave.

For this reason, from the moment of Addie's death Anse tries to be on his dignity, as befits the symbolic gain to be had in his social role. For this reason he carries reverence for Addie's body and his claims to self-reliance to the point of unintended self-caricature. For this reason, too, welcoming the newfound attention paid to him, Anse is on the lookout for more feathers with which to plume himself as the journey progresses.

Anse's reckless decision to cross the flooded river destroys his mule team and injures Cash. Anse senses that now he has a capital opportunity to double his symbolic profits by a display of persuasive power and self-sufficiency. First he wins a victory in principle by reducing Armstid to a readiness to lend him valuable replacement mules even though he has just destroyed his own through folly. Bypassing the mere practical profit here, Anse then attempts a further symbolic gain by winning the needed mules openly in the activity he has engaged in covertly all along: trading. Armstid describes Anse returning from his trade: "He looked kind of funny: kind of more hang-dog than common, and kind of proud too. Like he had done something he thought was cute but wasn't so sho now how other folks would take it. . . . 'I reckon Snopes aint the only man in this country that can drive a trade,' he said" (*AILD*, 175).

As Armstid says, this scene is "kind of funny," in both senses. Of course, Anse has just driven a ruinous trade, spending the symbolic value of Cash's graphophone and Jewel's horse and making his family dangerously beholden to the extent of a mortgage on their farm tools. Appalled, Armstid quickly makes an open offer of his mules and urges the family to leave Cash there to heal (*AILD*, 178). But Anse is indefatigable in wanting to look as good in other folks' eyes as at least part of him believes he looks in his own. Doubly and triply burdened now—but, like Don Quixote, increasingly triumphant in his own eyes—Anse takes his family on its bumbling, tragic way.

A number of further trades and trade-offs follow on the rest of the journey and in Jefferson—the Bundrens even get Dr. Peabody to do what he can for Cash's leg and then pay *them* (*AILD*, 240)—right up to the novel's punch-line trade in its final words. But the previous examples are probably sufficient to make the pattern clear. The basic pattern is that of the culture's story of sacred economics, translated into a secular strategy: the last shall be first; or, losing means winning in the end. Or, in other words, the habit is that of being so fixated on some envisioned ultimate reward that "pays in the long run" that you are distracted from weighing the losses and attrition you are suffering in the present.

Have you lost wife and mother? Have you traumatized the youngest member of the family by failing to give him comfort? Have you lost valuable mules? Have you physically handicapped son and brother? Have you mortgaged property you cannot afford to lose? Have you exposed the family, living and dead, to outrage and humiliation? Have you been sexually degraded by an unfeeling townsman? Have you failed to see, much less have, the red toy train? Have you impassively watched your son be institutionalized, and have you, ignoring what he will suffer, allowed your brother to be committed to a place where, as in the grave, there is "none of the bothering and such" (*AILD*, 221)?

No matter. Count your ultimate gains: a supposedly enhanced reputation for self-sufficiency, false teeth, a fierce-eyed, duck-shaped new Mrs. Bundren, a graphophone, a promise to Vardaman that next time they'll get him that train—and, as the final fruit of your sweat, bananas and "New Hope" (*AILD*, 107) for all. Not exactly liberty and justice for all, or anybody. But at least, it might be said, the family is facing toward the future with the evident desire to believe that somehow all their sweat has not been wasted, or at least won't be wasted "in the long run." As for the past, they have evidently put it behind them. Cash's sudden anticipation of the future solace of the graphophone allows his audibly inadequate requiem for Darl's death-in-life: "listening to it, I would think what a shame Darl couldn't be [note the slip for 'be *here*'] to enjoy it too. But it is better so for him. This world is not his world; this life his life" (*AILD*, 242). This world and this life open out before the Bundrens in the novel's last words. Anse, unable to look at the family he has neither consulted nor informed about his marriage, introduces the surprising future: " 'Meet Mrs Bundren,' he says."

But is the family facing toward the future in any but the trite sense that we all face that way until we die? And in fact, isn't it just the habit of facing too far and too exclusively forward that has been part of their problem, as it is their culture's? To face toward the future in the positive, concrete sense means to be better prepared to act in the present and future than in the past, to fulfill well-chosen desires and real needs. It means that the past has been neither written off nor eulogized away, but that one can remember it to learn from mistakes and to find past examples of effective thought and action and begin using them in the present to make a better future. It means, in short, that patterns of thought and action could, if necessary, be modified significantly or even broken. It would mean that the fragmented collective action represented by the Bundrens would coalesce.

What is there to confirm our hope of such an alteration within the purview of this fictional world? As Faulkner's career progresses, hope emerges more and more explicitly as perhaps the superlative virtue in his writing (which means that he questions it as well). Even more than the other traditional highest virtues of Faulkner's

Christian culture—love and faith—the main characteristic of hope is its ability to build itself on the most minimal possibilities. Given the particularly open quality of hope, not to mention the openness of Faulkner's novel, readers have found a variety of reasons either to hope or to rule out hope for these hill farmers of Yoknapatawpha. Perhaps one may speculate that, at this point in Faulkner's career, what hope there is rests on the continuing endurance of the people combined with the discontent, the outrage, that flares up in them. Together, perhaps their capacities for endurance and outrage suggest that the people might someday follow up on the best, constructive impulses of their symbolic action in giving their children such names as Vardaman. Then their new hope would be new and real.

# 8

# *Life after "Meet Mrs. Bundren":*
## *Looking Beyond*

It's a truism that readers will differ in summing up their sense of hope or lack of hope as well as their other reactions to this novel or any other text. One reason, I would suggest, has to do with differences we have learned in the focus of reading. Since reading habits are enmeshed in broader social practices, each focus of reading carries assumptions about the relationship between the symbolic activity of writing and reading and the practical consequences of this action. This final chapter will briefly make a few relevant assumptions explicit.

What I mean by the focus of reading can be shown by two examples. First, some readers give exclusive or primary weight to the fortunes of one or more of the characters or to the inferable possibilities of their further action in their fictional world. What has happened to the characters? And what is likely to happen to them, given what we have learned about them and the opportunities and limits of their novel's universe? This was our focus, more or less, at the end of the previous chapter.

Because much of "high" modern literature features characters who are severely limited or defeated by the constricted possibilities of their fictional worlds, readers who have learned only to focus their reading on character not uncommonly find these books depressing and avoid them.

But quite different conclusions may result from a second focus. We may give less weight to assessing the fates of the characters than to judging or understanding the author we may infer from the writing. Here our interest may be mainly biographical—the author as private man or woman—or aesthetic—the author as skilled (or unskilled) fabricator of these characters and their world. So, for example, a reader's sense that the characters inhabit a hopeless fictional world may be outweighed by exhilaration at the virtuosity of the author's performance in evoking this world. Such readers of *As I Lay Dying* might say not that the novel left them feeling hopeless but that it left them feeling elated at its artistic power, its tour de force in the best sense.

Some early reviewers of the novel offer examples of this attitude: they find in Faulkner's rich evocation of his characters a zest for life that outweighs the theme of death. For these readers, this artistic esprit counts heavily in their assessment of the book. Notice that other reviewers recognize a similar difference between author and characters but see it as a fault: "The quality of Mr. Faulkner's own mind . . . is of a high order; the quality of the minds of the people he chooses to set before you . . . is, on the contrary, of a very low sort."[14]

Setting aside other possibilities for reading emphasis, let us now make explicit the primary reading focus until now implicit in the preceding chapters and consider the perspective it offers, looking beyond the novel's ending.

The focus we have used is partly similar to both of those just described but is distinct from them. This approach weighs the fates of the characters in their world, and it seeks to appreciate the novel's technical virtuosity. But more important, it reads the novel as a feeling critique of the social order in which these characters move and have their being. Similarly, it reads the virtuoso artistic effects as ways to encompass the reader in this feeling critique at all levels, including the procedures of reading themselves.

The distinctive mark of this approach is that it grants both the implied author's critique and readers' possible engagement in it a place in the book's purview of society. In other words, the boundaries of the novel extend beyond the limits of the characters and what they can perceive, feel, and do, to include Faulkner's intelligence as a novelist and our intelligence as readers.

In this broader sense, Yoknapatawpha County is more than the address of the Bundrens, Tulls, Armstids, and the rest. This society is Faulkner's address and potentially ours as well, and we all may find our roles to play there. If the novel leaves us, for example, disheartened by the Bundrens and all that is bizarre and terrible in their society, but also more aware of some of the means by which effective collective action is diverted and dispersed, then this informed dissatisfaction on our part opens the possibility for social improvement as we discover analogues to or continuations of the troubles of Yoknapatawpha in our present world.

If the novel helps us to think and act beyond the Bundrens and their immediate society, then that too is part of the novel's open range of vision into the future. That too is one of the potentials of and in Yoknapatawpha, in its larger circumference that includes writer and reader as participants in ongoing social being. And, even more than Addie, Faulkner and his fictional county have indeed continued to speak and be spoken to in the cultural narratives and actions long after his physical death.

With this broadened focus for reading we have considered the book within both a regional (Southern) and a wider historical context of concerns as the twenties pass into the thirties. In this context of social transition, a distinctive twenties literary concern for the lonely individual's loss of community begins also to anticipate a distinctive thirties desire and need for collective action, prompted by the unblinkable circumstances of Southern and national—indeed, nearly worldwide—economic crisis. *As I Lay Dying* partakes of and responds to this dialectical combination of concerns.

*As I Lay Dying* is obviously not a full-fledged political novel, like John Dos Passos' *The Big Money* or Steinbeck's *The Grapes of Wrath,* if we mean by this term a novel that explicitly addresses the larger socioeconomic arena. We saw that Faulkner instead critically represents here what he elsewhere calls the three compulsions—religious, economic, and political—as they interact at stress points linking private and public life, from psyche to family to society. This critique is less concerned with this or that cooperative action than it is with specific ways in which fruitful action is diverted into poor substitutes. The heroically bizarre burial journey epitomizes this diversion, with its clannish privacy, conventions of exaggerated individualism, largely unproductive class and gender discontents, and hints of parallel distortions in racism—in short, with all its representations of the social ties that bind people in the tensions of enforced apartness.

What is deeply political about this book is the novelistic intelligence that does its thinking in and through fiction and on this basis detects the culture's master storytelling that shapes these burdened social ties. Thus Faulkner's continuing literary interest in the growth of stories out of stories, which becomes most explicit in his later novel *Absalom, Absalom!*, is inseparable from the social and political concerns of *As I Lay Dying*. The novel is similarly political in provoking readers to trace this webbing of narratives further, into their own extensions and parallels. This further tracing isn't simply, or mainly, a matter of following an allegory in which the references to Vardaman and Whitfield, say, lead us unerringly to the progressive features of their politics as the ultimate or necessary stopping point for the reader's intelligence. Rather it's a question of readers' taking a cue from the novel's demonstration that everyone's stories are to be completed by others' stories, and that even master storytelling may be made available to critical inspection.

Especially if the novel is read within the context of thirties concerns, the question, finally, is whether the symbolic action that is the book itself will contribute to further effective action of some kind. The alternative is that it will become another, secularized version of the sacred economics it critiques, a dead-end diversion of action sealed in the reader's "ultimate secret place" of imagination. Faulkner's emergence later in his career as a public figure calling for cooperative action on public issues perhaps indicates his own nonliterary response, though belated, to some of the questions and implications of this pivotal novel and of his subsequent writings.

A book can propose such questions, but it cannot dictate the answers. We as readers are the answerers, the novel's own future.

# notes and references

1. *Essays, Speeches & Public Letters by William Faulkner*, ed. James B. Meriwether (New York: Random House, 1966), 181; hereafter cited in text. On Faulkner's "No to death," see Warwick Wadlington, *Reading Faulknerian Tragedy* (Ithaca: Cornell University Press, 1987).

2. Frederick L. Gwynn and Joseph L. Blotner, eds., *Faulkner in the University* (Charlottesville: University Press of Virginia, 1978), 74; hereafter cited in text.

3. For Faulkner's revisionary activity, see Richard C. Moreland, *Faulkner and Modernism: Rereading and Rewriting* (Madison: University of Wisconsin Press, 1990).

4. William Faulkner, "Introduction for *The Sound and the Fury*," *Southern Review*, n.s., 8 (1972): 709. For further details on the composition of the novel, see Dianne L. Cox, "Introduction," in *William Faulkner's "As I Lay Dying": A Critical Casebook* (New York: Garland, 1985).

5. Carvel Collins, "Faulkner and Mississippi," *University of Mississippi Studies in English* 15 (1978): 159.

6. "An Introduction to *The Sound and the Fury*," in *A Faulkner Miscellany*, 158, ed. James B. Meriwether (Jackson: University Press of Mississippi, 1974). This is a second introduction Faulkner wrote to the earlier novel and should not be confused with the one cited in note 4.

7. William Faulkner, *As I Lay Dying* (New York: Vintage, 1987), 103, 173, 174; hereafter cited in text as *AILD*.

8. William Faulkner, *The Sound and the Fury* (New York: Random House, 1984), 87.

9. *The New Deal and the South*, ed. James C. Cobb and Michael V. Namorato (Jackson: University Press of Mississippi, 1984), 5.

10. John Ray Skates, *Mississippi: A Bicentennial History* (New York: Norton, 1979), 127–33; hereafter cited in text. For the fullest account, see George Coleman Osborn, *James Kimble Vardaman: Southern Commoner* (Jackson: Hederman Brothers, 1981); William F. Holmes, *The White Chief: James Kimble Vardaman* (Baton Rouge: Louisiana State University Press, 1970); and Albert D. Kirwan, *Revolt of the Rednecks: Mississippi Politics, 1876–1925* (Lexington: University of Kentucky Press, 1951).

11. William Faulkner, "The Big Shot," in *Uncollected Stories of William Faulkner*, 508, ed. Joseph Blotner (New York: Vintage, 1981).

12. This discussion is partly indebted to a somewhat different analysis of this scene by John T. Matthews, "*As I Lay Dying* in the Machine Age," *Boundary 2* (1992).

13. Bill R. Baker, *Catch the Vision: The Life of Henry L. Whitfield of Mississippi* (Jackson: University Press of Mississippi), 15–39, 40–59, 67–75, 78–81, 86–110, 132–33, 148.

14. "A Witch's Brew: *As I Lay Dying*," *New York Times Book Review*, 19 October 1930, 6.

# bibliography

## PRIMARY WORKS

### Selected Prose Fiction

The following titles are listed in order of date of initial publication. See the chronology for original publication dates.

*Soldiers' Pay.* New York: Liveright, 1954.
*Mosquitoes.* New York: Liveright, 1955.
*Sartoris.* New York: Random House, 1966.
*The Sound and the Fury.* New York: Vintage, 1987.
*As I Lay Dying.* New York: Vintage, 1987.
*Sanctuary.* New York: Vintage, 1967.
*Light in August.* New York: Vintage, 1990.
*Pylon.* New York: Vintage, 1987.
*Absalom, Absalom!* New York: Vintage, 1987.
*The Unvanquished.* New York: Vintage, 1965.
*The Wild Palms.* New York: Vintage, 1964.
*The Hamlet.* New York: Vintage, 1956.
*Go Down, Moses.* New York: Vintage, 1973.
*Intruder in the Dust.* New York: Vintage, 1972.
*Collected Stories of William Faulkner.* New York: Vintage, 1977.
*Requiem for a Nun.* New York: Vintage, 1975.
*A Fable.* New York: Vintage, 1978.
*The Town.* New York: Vintage, 1961.
*The Mansion.* New York: Vintage, 1959.
*The Reivers.* New York: Vintage, 1962.
*Flags in the Dust.* New York: Vintage, 1974.
*Sanctuary: The Original Text.* Edited by Noel Polk. New York: Random House, 1981.

### Collections, Interviews, and Letters

*Essays, Speeches & Public Letters.* Edited by James B. Meriwether. New York: Random House, 1966.

Faulkner in the University: Class Conferences at the University of Virginia, 1957–58. Edited by Frederick L. Gwynn and Joseph L. Blotner. Charlottesville: University Press of Virginia, 1978.

Lion in the Garden: Interviews with William Faulkner, 1926–1962. Edited by James B. Meriwether and Michael Millgate. Lincoln: University of Nebraska Press, 1980.

Selected Letters of William Faulkner. Edited by Joseph Blotner. New York: Random House, 1977.

William Faulkner Manuscripts 7: "As I Lay Dying." Edited by Thomas L. McHaney. New York: Garland, 1987. Holograph manuscript and carbon typescript of the novel.

## SECONDARY WORKS

### Books

Adams, Richard P. Faulkner: Myth and Motion, 71–84. Princeton: Princeton University Press, 1968. Mythic death and rebirth patterns in the novel, which is defined as a kind of pastoral elegy.

Bleikasten, André. Faulkner's "As I Lay Dying." Rev. ed. Translated by Roger Little. Bloomington: Indiana University Press, 1973. A comprehensive book-length introduction to the novel as representing the radical contingency and finitude of human existence. One of the most influential studies of the novel.

_____. The Ink of Melancholy: Faulkner's Novels from "The Sound and the Fury" to "Light in August," 149–209. Bloomington: Indiana University Press, 1990. Condenses and updates this critic's earlier study by drawing on and extending existing commentary.

Blotner, Joseph. Faulkner: A Biography. New York: Random House, 1984. Deals primarily with Faulkner's life.

Brooks, Cleanth. William Faulkner: The Yoknapatawpha Country, 141–66, 398–401. New Haven: Yale University Press, 1963. The novel as an examination of the heroic act. One of the most influential studies of Faulkner.

Capps, Jack L. "As I Lay Dying": A Concordance to the Novel. Ann Arbor: University Microfilms International, 1977. A basic resource for study of the novel.

Cox, Dianne L. William Faulkner's "As I Lay Dying": A Critical Casebook. New York: Garland, 1985. Anthology of significant essays, with an introduction by Cox. Especially noteworthy are essays by Bedient on isolation, Branch on analogies to modern painting, Garrison on the Bundrens' failure to see themselves as active agents, and Ross on verb tense and psychological time.

Fowler, Doreen. Faulkner's Changing Vision: From Outrage to Affirmation, 23–26. Ann Arbor: UMI Research Press, 1983. Argues that the novel is

Bibliography

typical of Faulkner's early writings in representing human existence as
an outrage perpetrated by nature and by human beings.

Friedman, Alan Warren. *William Faulkner*, 75–88. New York: Frederick
Ungar, 1984. Weighs pros and cons about the novel. Pairs it with *Light
in August* as atypical Faulkner texts.

Gresset, Michoel. *Fascination: Faulkner's Fiction, 1919–1936*, 215–28.
Translated by Thomas West. Durham: Duke University Press, 1989.
Outrage and the experience of seeing. Draws on Sartre.

Howe, Irving. *William Faulkner: A Critical Study*, 52–56, 175–91. 3d ed.
Chicago: University of Chicago Press, 1975. Judges the novel to be
Faulkner's kindliest, most affectionate.

Irwin, John T. *Doubling and Incest/Repetition and Revenge: A Speculative
Reading of Faulkner*, 53–55. Baltimore: Johns Hopkins University
Press, 1975. Uses similarities with *The Sound and the Fury* to argue for
Darl's incestuous attraction to Dewey Dell. A Freudian-Nietzschean
interpretation of Faulkner.

Kartiganer, Donald M. *The Fragile Thread: The Meaning of Form in Faulkner's
Novels*, 23–33. Amherst: University of Massachusetts Press, 1979.
Compares Darl and Cash and argues that the novel partly fails because
plot works against consciousness.

Kinney, Arthur F. *Faulkner's Narrative Poetics: Style as Vision*, 161–77.
Amherst: University of Massachusetts Press, 1978. A study of the
novel's narrative consciousness that concentrates on Darl and Addie.

Levins, Lynn Gartrell. *Faulkner's Heroic Design: The Yoknapatawpha Novels*,
94–114. Athens: University of Georgia Press, 1976. The theme of heroism as found in the novel's analogues to epic journey and religious
pilgrimage.

Lockyer, Judith. *Ordered by Words: Language and Narration in the Novels of
William Faulkner*, 72–85. Carbondale: Southern Illinois University
Press, 1991. The novel as a contemplation of the contextual and rela-
tional nature of language.

Luce, Dianne C. *"As I Lay Dying" Annotated.* New York: Garland, 1990. A
companion to the novel that clarifies difficult words, dialect, allusions,
and historical events.

Matthews, John T. *The Play of Faulkner's Language*, 40–42. Ithaca: Cornell
University Press, 1982. Uses Addie's soliloquy to argue for Faulkner's
commitment to writing as a place beyond the spoken word. Interpretation of Faulkner draws on deconstructionist theories.

Millgate, Michael. *The Achievement of William Faulkner*, 104–22. New York:
Random House, 1966. A broad introduction to the novel.

Minter, David. *William Faulkner: His Life and Work.* Baltimore: Johns Hopkins University Press, 1980. The relations between Faulkner's life and
works.

Morris, Wesley, with Barbara Alverson Morris. *Reading Faulkner*, 9–16,
28–35, 150–75. Madison: University of Wisconsin Press, 1989. The

117

political dimensions of Faulkner's writing. Uses Lacanian analysis to argue that the novel shows the limits of the symbolic order and masculine mastery.

Parker, Robert Dale. *Faulkner and the Novelistic Imagination*, 23–58. Urbana and Chicago: University of Illinois Press, 1985. Argues that the novel presents contrary possibilities to postpone interpretation and that the characters' secretiveness is related to the "primal secret" of uncertain knowledge.

Powers, Lyall H. *Faulkner's Yoknapatawpha Comedy*, 50–72. Ann Arbor: University of Michigan Press, 1980. The Bundrens as manifestations of the goodness of simple people; their difficulty in facing death and their "second chance" at the novel's conclusion.

Reed, Joseph W., Jr. *Faulkner's Narrative*, 84–111, 283. New Haven: Yale University Press, 1973. Relates imagery, themes (especially that of becoming), and narrative.

Robinson, Fred Miller. *The Comedy of Language: Studies in Modern Comic Literature*, 51–88. Amherst: University of Massachusetts Press, 1980. The novel's complex Bergsonian comedy.

Ross, Stephen M. *Fiction's Inexhaustible Voice: Speech and Writing in Faulkner*, 65–67, 111–29. Athens: University of Georgia Press, 1989. Examines the novel's play with the illusion of speech, as part of a study of Faulkner's fictional "voice."

Slatoff, Walter J. *Quest for Failure*, 158–73. Ithaca: Cornell University Press, 1960. Argues that intractable ambiguities and obscurities in the novel illustrate Faulkner's weakness as a writer.

Snead, James A. *Figures of Division: William Faulkner's Major Novels*, 45–80. New York and London: Methuen, 1986. The novel as a critique of convention, in the divisive exchanges and substitutions of language, society, and the family.

Stonum, Gary Lee. *Faulkner's Career: An Internal Literary History*, 94–122. Ithaca: Cornell University Press, 1979. The novel as an attempt to represent life's motion, contrasted to the fixed categories of knowledge and morality.

Sundquist, Eric J. *Faulkner: The House Divided*, 28–43. Baltimore: Johns Hopkins University Press, 1983. Analogies between the ritual expression of grief, the illusions of identity, and the form of the novel. Compassion and love expressed in comedy.

Vickery, Olga. *The Novels of William Faulkner: A Critical Interpretation*, 50–65. Baton Rouge: Louisiana State University Press, 1959. Addie and her effects on her children; argues that Cash matures through suffering. Influential early study of the novel.

Wadlington, Warwick. *Reading Faulknerian Tragedy*, 101–30. Ithaca: Cornell University Press, 1987. The novel compared to a purposely defective death rite, as part of the development of Faulkner's modern tragedy within the context of an honor-shame culture.

# Bibliography

Waggoner, Hyatt. *William Faulkner: From Jefferson to the World*, 62–87. Lexington: University of Kentucky Press, 1959. Christian themes, imagery, and characterization.

Williams, David. *Faulkner's Women: The Myth and the Muse*, 97–126. Montreal: McGill-Queen's University Press, 1977. Addie and Dewey Dell as archetypes of death and the mother.

Wittenberg, Judith Bryant. *Faulkner: The Transfiguration of Biography*, 103–17. Lincoln: University of Nebraska Press, 1979. Biographical connections to the combined characters of the Bundren brothers.

Wright, Austin M. *Recalcitrance, Faulkner, and the Professors: A Critical Fiction*. Iowa City: University of Iowa Press, 1990. A fictional symposium that uses the novel to argue for an updated formalist approach to literature. Sees the effect of the novel as that of wonder.

## Articles

See the Cox anthology above for many of the best articles on the novel.

Collins, Carvel. "The Pairing of *The Sound and the Fury* and *As I Lay Dying*." *Princeton University Library Chronicle* 18 (1957): 114–23. Influential early article revealing source of Faulkner's title and tracing myth patterns and Greek parallels in the novels.

Hemenway, Robert. "Enigmas of Being in *As I Lay Dying*." *Modern Fiction Studies* 16 (1970): 133–46. Detailed analysis of Darl's "emptying for sleep" passage and his discussion of "is" and "are" with Vardaman.

Kartiganer, Donald M. "The Farm and the Journey: Ways of Mourning and Meaning in *As I Lay Dying*." *Mississippi Quarterly* 43 (1990): 251–303. The interplay of stasis and motion, being and becoming, in the novel's language and narrative form.

Lilly, Paul R., Jr. "Caddy and Addie: Speakers of Faulkner's Impeccable Language." *Journal of Narrative Technique* 3 (1973): 170–82. Uses similarities with *The Sound and the Fury* to relate the form of the novel to Faulkner's concept of poetry as a transcendence of language.

Matthews, John T. "*As I Lay Dying* in the Machine Age." *Boundary 2* (1992). Reads the novel in relation to the technology and commodification of modern life.

Simon, John K. "What Are You Laughing At, Darl?: Madness and Humor in *As I Lay Dying*." *College English* 25 (1963): 104–10. Darl as a consistent character, and his laughter as a commentary on dehumanized people.

# index

# The Author

Warwick Wadlington is Joan Negley Kelleher Centennial Professor in the Department of English at the University of Texas at Austin. He is the author of *The Confidence Game in American Literature* (1975), *Reading Faulknerian Tragedy* (1987), and articles and papers on nineteenth- and twentieth-century American literature.